MANIFEST A JOY-FILLED RELATIONSHIP

USING UNIVERSAL LAWS TO CREATE
YOUR DESIRED RELATIONSHIP

JASON & TINA MARIE SCOTT

Manifest A Joy-Filled Relationship

Copyright © 2024 by Jason & Tina Marie Scott

All rights reserved. Printed in the United States of America. No part of this book or any portion thereof may be used or reproduced in any manner whatsoever without the express written permission of the publisher except for the use of brief quotations embodied in critical articles and reviews. Names have been altered to safeguard client confidentiality.

Principles Work
430 E. 162nd St STE 252
South Holland, IL 60473
legendaryrelationship.com

First Printing, 2024
ISBN 979-8-9910034-3-8 (Hardback)
ISBN 979-8-9910034-0-7 (Paperback)
ISBN 979-8-9910034-1-4 (eBook)
ISBN 979-8-9910034-2-1 (Audiobook)

Library of Congress Catalog Number: 2024915553

Ordering Information

Special discounts are available for bulk purchases by corporations, associations, and other groups. For more details, visit legendaryrelationship.com or email us at team@legendaryrelationship.com

CONTENTS

Introduction 1

1. The Law of Oneness 13
2. The Law of Vibration 41
3. The Law of Inspired Action 63
4. The Law of Correspondence 95
5. The Law of Cause and Effect 124
6. The Law of Attraction 152
7. The Law of Compensation 176
8. The Law of Perpetual Transmutation of Energy 192
9. The Law of Relativity 206
10. The Law of Polarity 238
11. The Law of Rhythm 253
12. The Law of Gender 268

About the Authors 295

INTRODUCTION

Welcome to the illuminating exploration of *Manifest a Joy-filled Relationship: Using Universal Laws to Create Your Desired Relationship.*

Imagine this: You find yourself caught in the turbulent currents of a relationship storm, your heart weighed down by the gravity of constant unresolved conflicts and emotional turbulence. The pain is intense, a knot in your chest tightening with every strained conversation and misunderstood gesture. The ache is not just emotional; it's a deep-seated longing for harmony and understanding, a desire for connection unmarred by the current chaos. This yearning goes beyond mere emotion; it's a profound longing for tranquility and recaptured intimacy.

Here's the promise of potential pleasure that lies ahead: Picture a relationship where understanding flows effortlessly, conflicts transform into opportunities for growth, and love becomes a harmonious exchange rather than a constant battle. In the intricate unknowns of existence, a set of timeless principles govern the very essence of our reality - The 12 Laws of the Universe. As you discover these universal principles, you will witness the extreme interplay between your thoughts, beliefs, and the circumstances in your life. Envision a life where the 12 Laws of the Universe act as your guiding compass, steering you towards a profound connection that transcends the ordinary and taps into the extraordinary. Each law is a unique facet of this cosmic gem, revealing insights into the nature of reality, consciousness, and the interconnectedness of all things. From the Law of Attraction, which teaches you about the power of your thoughts and emotions in shaping your experiences, to the Law of Cause and Effect, which emphasizes the complex web of consequences stemming from your actions, these laws serve as a rule of thumb for conscious living and healthier relationships.

In the expansive landscape of human relationships, where emotions ebb and flow and the echoes of connection reverberate, the purpose of this book is not merely a theoretical discourse on esoteric principles; it is a practical guide, a roadmap that empowers you to navigate the complicated terrain of your relationship with purpose and intention. By applying the insights collected from the 12 Universal Laws, we aim to equip you with the tools to transform your relationships into vibrant, fulfilling expressions of connection. It is an invitation to embark on a transformative journey - that transcends the ordinary dynamics of relationships and ushers you into a realm where conscious co-creation becomes your driving force.

Let us introduce ourselves - Jason and Tina Marie, practitioners of Universal Truths, eager to accompany you on this profound journey toward harmonious relationships. Drawing upon our diverse backgrounds in coaching, psychology, metaphysics, theoretical physics, fundamental science, practical Christianity, and life experiences, we embarked upon this quest a quarter century ago to unravel the secrets that could enrich and fortify our connection and save our marriage.

This book is one of the many fruits of our labor - a mixture of ancient wisdom and practical application that possesses the transformative power to enrich not only your connection with your partner but all your connections. Our intention behind this exploration is twofold: to empower you with the knowledge of the 12 Universal Laws and to inspire you to facilitate profound transformations within your relationships through the understanding and application of these laws.

As you begin your journey through the pages of our book, our primary objective is to serve as a guiding light, illuminating your path to loving and conscious connections. Let us reshape the essence of your connections together using the invaluable wisdom encapsulated within the 12 Universal Laws.

This book is not a set of rules to follow but rather a flexible guide, inviting you to adopt an understanding that goes beyond surface-level interactions and dig deep into the energetic undercurrents that shape the quality of our relationships. The purpose is to facilitate a paradigm shift from perceiving relationships as sheer chance encounters to recognizing them as intentional, energetic exchanges that can be consciously molded and nurtured. Hence, by embracing the universal truths contained within these laws, you become an active participant in co-creating a relationship that resonates with authenticity, love, and shared growth.

Practicality is at the core of our purpose. We aim to bridge the gap between theory and application through insightful exercises, relatable real-life examples, and reflective practices. The wisdom in the 12 Universal Laws is a living, breathing force that you can harness to transform how you relate to others and, in turn, how others relate to you—freeing you from the erroneous belief that destiny controls your relationship, that will inevitably lead to disharmony and unhappiness. Become aware that the power lies within you, not outside of you.

Nevertheless, the importance of this exploration also extends beyond the realms of philosophy. Scientific studies across disciplines such as psychology, neuroscience, and quantum physics increasingly highlight the interconnected nature of all things. What was once considered mystical or esoteric is now converging with empirical evidence, forming an undeniable link between the scientific and the spiritual worlds.

As we unfold the layers of each law, our goal is to empower you to navigate the nuances of relationships with intentionality and mindfulness. We invite you to explore the energetic frequencies you bring to your connections, understand the mirrors relationships provide through the Law of Correspondence, and consciously align your actions with your aspirations through the Law of Inspired Action.

As you turn the pages and immerse yourself in the forthcoming chapters, don't merely read but engage actively with the material. Consider this a call to action—an opportunity to embrace the transformative power of the 12 Laws of the Universe and integrate them to unlock a profound sense of fulfillment and joy in your relationship.

Each chapter of this book takes you deeper into the orderly knowledge of the laws, providing practical insights, exercises, and real-life examples to guide you toward harmonious relationships. Through this exploration, you will gain the tools to transcend limitations, manifest your desires, and cultivate deeper, more meaningful connections. Are you ready? The journey starts now with a commitment to understanding, applying, and embodying these cosmic principles. Welcome to your personal journey viewed through the lens of the 12 Universal

INTRODUCTION

Laws, encouraging self-discovery, conscious connection, and endless possibilities.

Are you sure you are ready, willing, and committed to this universal adventure? Have you put aside old feelings, beliefs, and discontents? Are you open and receptive to what the universe may have for you? We invite you to unburden yourself and leave all your preconceived ideas behind. We ask that you enter this odyssey with a free, open, and receptive mind. Did you dispose of all pre-filled conscious and unconscious mind-containers? You can rest assured that they will be filled with better-equipped treasures of the universe to help you see things from a different perspective that will assist you in navigating your life and relationship(s) - once you have successfully completed your mission- the book.

∞∞∞

Your journey begins with ***The Law of Divine Oneness***, the foundational principle and the beginning of our relational understanding.

Here, we can't emphasize enough that everything and everyone in the universe connects at the deepest level and that the well-being of one is intricately tied to the well-being of all. As you take your first steps anxiously anticipating the exploration of this chapter, consider a moment in your life when you felt isolated, disconnected, or misunderstood in your relationship. It may have been an argument that left you both wounded and lonely despite being physically in each other's presence.

Now, imagine you have a deeper understanding of the interconnectedness of all things, especially how it applies to you and your partner. Your pain becomes a shared experience, magnifying your joy through the cosmic web that binds you. By using the practices within the Law of Divine Oneness, you obtain the power to transform isolation into unity and build a relationship that thrives. Through your willingness to change, you realize that interconnectedness is a crucial piece in laying the foundation for compassion, empathy, and a sense of shared responsibility in your relationship(s).

Next, your travel brings you to the land where **The Law of Vibration** takes center stage, highlighting the energetic frequencies that underlie your interactions. We ask that you envision a scenario where your emotions and thoughts are like notes in an intergalactic symphony. When disagreeing, energies disrupt the harmony, and conflicts arise. Picture a moment when your energy clashed with your partner's, creating a dissonance that reverberated throughout your relationship. Was it intentional? Probably not. However, without awareness, this clash can continue a destructive course, destroying everything in its path.

Now, picture the pleasure of understanding the Law of Vibration. Through this knowledge, you can attune your emotional frequencies to create a harmonious resonance with your mate and those around you. In this land, you learn to navigate the vibrational ballads of emotions, transforming discord into beautiful, orchestrated melodies of connection and understanding.

Then, you swim across the river of **The Law of Inspired Action**. It invites you to rise above passive observation and actively participate in co-creating a fulfilling relationship. You can't just look at the water; you must jump in and swim. If you are open-minded, you will discover the power of inspired action to propel your relationship forward. There are many ways in which your conscious efforts can align with the cosmic forces at play, bringing your vision into manifestation and transforming your relationship into a living, breathing expression of your deepest desires.

Think of your vision for your relationship - the dream of connection, growth, and fulfillment. Yet, despite your desires, you feel stuck, unsure of the steps to take to turn your vision into reality. The Law of Inspired Action teaches us that intention alone is not enough; action is the bridge between dreams and manifestation. You will be encouraged to recognize growth opportunities, express love through intentional actions, and align your behaviors with the kind of connections you wish to exhibit.

The river currents float you along its chosen course into **The Law of Correspondence**, which becomes a mirror reflecting the dynamics within your relationship. In this chapter, you discover pliable solutions to breaking free from destructive cycles. By recognizing the correspondence between your internal and external worlds, you gain the power to shift the dynamics of your relationship and bring about positive, maintainable change.

Consider a time when you felt trapped in a cycle of repetitive arguments or patterns in your relationship - an issue that seemed to be on "repeat" mode. The Law of Correspondence teaches us that what occurs in the microcosm of our relationships reflects in the universe's macrocosm. In other words, "As above, so below; as below, so above." Correspondence tells you the dynamics you encounter in your connections with your partner is a mirror reflecting the dynamics within yourself. By observing the reflections of universal truths in your everyday life, you gain awareness of the greater cosmic order that guides your journey. Here, you will acquire valuable insights into the root causes of your relational challenges and use universal keys to restore balance and understanding.

You begin to chart a different course using **The Law of Cause and Effect**. This law reminds us that every action has a reaction, and every choice carries consequences that travel through our connections, irrespective of its type. Reflect on moments when you've witnessed the consequences of your actions or words on your relationship that yielded negative results.

Here, you are encouraged to make conscious choices that align with the love and passion you seek. Only then will you be able to witness the positive effects that manifest when you become a conscious creator in your relationship dynamics, shedding new light on your role, not your partner's, in the Law of Cause and Effect.

Nevertheless, due to your conscious choices, the waters begin to rage as **The Law of Attraction** tosses you to and fro. You cry out, 'Wait! I only want to attract good!' But the raging waters insist that you recognize its hidden power. Consequently, within the context of relationships, this law compels you to examine the current state of your relationship. You must decide whether to continue attracting more of what you currently experience or shift and change to allow and attract what you truly desire. This process helps you uncover the decisive role of your thoughts and emotions in shaping the quality of your connection. Like magnets, our energies attract similar frequencies, influencing the nature of the relationships we cultivate. The Law of Attraction reveals the profound truth that like

INTRODUCTION

attracts like. Your thoughts, emotions, and intentions act as magnets, shaping the experiences that become visible in your life and relationship.

This law serves as a profound guide to intentional relationship building. In this chapter, you discover how to channel the magnetic power of your consciousness to manifest the relationship you desire. You uncover the secrets – are they really secrets? – of intentional creation, attraction, and building emotional, physical, and spiritual connections that align with your highest aspirations for your relationship.

Meanwhile, uncertainty grips you from the stormy waves, erasing your charted course. Your thoughts race with worry as **The Law of Compensation** influences you to see how your contributions shape your current relational landscape. This law suggests that you are not fooled by what you think you are giving to your relationship from your perspective. This chapter proposes that the universe responds to your thoughts, feelings, and actions by providing compensation in kind. Attuning to this law becomes pivotal for the awareness of illusory and factual giving and receiving that contribute to your relationship goals and desires.

The rift then pulls you into **The Law of Perpetual Transmutation of Energy**, revealing the transformative power within your experiences. In this chapter, the law gently nudges you to maintain positive thoughts, intentions, actions, and reactions despite your current situation.

Consider when you invested time, energy, and effort into your relationship, only to feel your labors went unnoticed or unreciprocated. It was a time when negative energy seemed to engulf your relationship, casting a shadow over the once-bright outlook for your future. Where one negative thought led to another, then another, then another. By absorbing this law, you increase your ability to transmute negative energy or thought into positive growth and evolution.

The strong river currents of life continue to pull you along in unknown directions. What's that? You somehow spot an olive branch. You reach out to prevent yourself from becoming an unwilling participant in the rift's pull. No matter what, do not give up. Why? Because. Throughout this book, you are continually provided with practical tools and techniques, much like the branch, to shift the energy within your relationship and get back on course. You learn how to regain control by witnessing the alchemical process that turns challenges into opportunities, darkness into light, and discord into a catalyst for positive change.

Finally, you can rest and celebrate a victory! You have reached the riverbank past the halfway point. However, your journey is far from over. Up ahead, you see the treacherous mountains of the chapters of **The Laws of Relativity, Polarity, and Rhythm**, where you will find tools for navigating the diverse landscapes and terrains of your relationship journey. As you climb higher, you can see moments in your relationship when challenges seemed overwhelming, yet times when love felt endless. In other instances, your opposing opinions seemed to clash, creating continual tension and conflict. Even moments where your relationship rhythm experienced incredible highs and earth-shaking lows, creating unbalanced emotions of closeness and distance. Whether dealing with challenges, appreciating differences, or finding balance, it is in those chapters that

INTRODUCTION

you will find solace. Therefore, remember to keep reading. Knowledge is power but applied knowledge warrants results.

Ultimately, we want you to see your relationship in a new light. At this point, you have reached the climax. You can successfully look ahead, knowing that your journey is approaching its end. You look up to see how the stars uniformly align in the sky as they shed light upon the universe, revealing your path. You loosen your grip, knowing the rest of your journey will be smooth sailing. You have now arrived at ***The Law of Gender***. This is your last stop, where you learn how your masculine and feminine energies complement each other. Standing at your final destination, you see a movie playing across the dark, starry sky. This movie shows a time in your past when you fought against understanding and honoring the masculine and feminine aspects within yourself and your partner, leading to discord and disconnect. As the movie ends, a door opens and leads you down a corridor to explore how understanding and harmonizing these energies can enhance your connection.

How different would some of your most challenging experiences have been if you knew they only came to strengthen your relationship? As the old saying goes, "hindsight is 20/20." This means the phenomenon of looking back and seeing things differently or clearly after they have occurred, which we couldn't see at that time. Could your outcomes have been different? Could your thoughts, actions, and emotions have been expressed better, allowing the challenge to come and go without threatening the very essence of your bond? It is through understanding and harmonizing your energies that the true depth and richness of your connections are enhanced.

As you use and express the twelve universal laws, may your life resonate with the sweet melodies of love, wisdom, and unity. May you learn to enjoy your relationship with grace and understanding, recognizing the profound interconnectedness of all things and aligning yourself with the highest frequencies of existence.

The universe is waiting to reveal its secrets and transform the lives of those who seek to understand and apply its timeless laws!

So, as previously asked, "Are you ready to explore the great laws of the universe and transform your connections with your partner?" Adventure awaits! Turn the page and embrace your undiscovered connections and untapped potential.

Chapter One
THE LAW OF ONENESS
The Foundation of Relationships

As you venture into the foundational principles of the 12 Universal Laws, your exploration begins with the Law of Divine Oneness, which is rooted in ancient wisdom and stretches across many spiritual traditions throughout the world. This law speaks to the interconnectedness of all existence. This law asserts that you and everything in the universe are profoundly and highly interconnected. From the smallest particles to the grandest celestial bodies, all aspects of the universe are interconnected, extending beyond the physical realm to thoughts, emotions, and energies. Awareness of this law prompts you to recognize that separateness is an illusion and that we are all integral parts of a vast, interlinked cosmic structure, especially in your relationship.

It is in the quiet expanses of the universe where the stars give off glimmers of cosmic wonder, where you will find the Law of Divine Oneness directing the grand symphony of your interconnectedness. This law summons you to recognize the invisible energy that binds every living being, every particle of matter, and every breath of wind into a balanced life of existence. This law extends beyond individual lives to shape the collective consciousness of the planet. Every act of thoughtfulness, compassion, or discord contributes to the evolution of global consciousness. Thus, as you apply this law to your relationship, you will see how every act of kindness or selfishness, love or hate, and understanding or misunderstanding adds to the evolution of your relational consciousness.

When you acknowledge the power of this law, you participate in a reflective journey of recognition—recognizing that you and your partner's individual and collective lives are intertwined. As you unravel the mysteries of this law, you discover that your relationship is far from an isolated entity. Your relationship is meant to exhibit oneness and, therefore, represents the very essence of this law. Once understood and applied, this law becomes one of your most invaluable relationship tools, worth more than any possession you could ever acquire.

When you wholeheartedly embrace the Law of Divine Oneness, you develop a deeper sense of connection, understanding, and soundness in your relationship. Therefore, by choosing higher vibrational frequencies, you learn to maneuver troubling occurrences successfully and minimize their negative effects on your relationship and life. When you open up to universal oneness and engage in practical developmental exercises, self-reflection, and open communication, you unlock the transformative power within to create a more elevated and enlightened union.

∞∞∞∞

You must realize that every one of your actions, thoughts, or feelings has a ripple effect that extends far beyond its immediate presence. Therefore, every action, thought, or feeling you choose to do, think, or have affects your partner and shapes your relationship.

THE LAW OF ONENESS

This law becomes prominent as you begin to shift your perspective and view your relationship choices through the lens of oneness, not separateness. It's about becoming aware of the importance of releasing anger and negative feelings due to their possible rippling and far-reaching effects on your relationship. Awareness is significant as it establishes your willingness to express empathy and compassion as better options.

Look at your current relationship dynamics. Are you and your partner operating with an awareness of interconnectedness or separateness? You must recognize that your conscious choices support one or the other. You can operate out of unity once you realize your oneness to each other and the relationship. This unity holds the potential to mend rifts, strengthen bonds, and elevate you to a heightened state of relational awareness. You resolve conflicts through empathy and dialogue while learning to embrace mutual responsibility for the wellbeing of your shared environment. This law supports your harmonious coexistence by highlighting how your actions and expressions contribute to your relationship's overall joy. True happiness doesn't require compromising your wants and needs; it involves creating an authentic relationship where partners get what they need to flourish.

∞∞∞

The first law provides a framework for navigating challenges by attuning yourself to a higher frequency. This higher frequency is essential for you to become emotionally aware and present. Present in your ability to identify the interplay of polarities, the positive and negative forces. When you begin to welcome these differences, you can find balance and synergy to help you transcend challenges through mutual understanding and acceptance. By aligning your energies, you can overcome obstacles more quickly through the knowledge of universal oneness.

This law helps to regulate the ebb and flow of your energies that shape your relational reality. It dictates the connection of all things, emphasizing the elaborate interchange of energy and matter. This law allows you to tap into the universal flow that binds you and your partner, encouraging unity through your words, actions, and shared experiences. When you discover the underlying forces of energy exchange within your relationship, you see how the first law emphasizes the give-and-take essential for sustaining a healthy partnership. You realize that the exchange of your energy forms the foundation for building a lasting connection and the framework for manifesting a joyous relationship.

In the context of your relationship, this law indicates that the connection between you and your partner is not superficial but deeply intertwined within your existence. Therefore, the law becomes particularly powerful as you work through and gain insight into your relationship challenges. Instead of viewing conflicts as isolated events, you should approach them as opportunities for growth and mutual understanding. You recognize the sacredness of your connection and honor the intrinsic unity between you. By acknowledging that your actions and reactions ring through your shared energetic field, you develop a more empathetic and collaborative approach to problem-solving. You can face challenges together, viewing them as collective obstacles rather than divisive ones. Embracing the concept of universal oneness means that you and your partner now stand united against relationship disputes instead of on opposing sides.

∞∞∞

Psychological and sociological studies offer valuable insights into human behavior and societal dynamics. These studies analyze the impact separateness and negative choices have on relationships. This research stresses the importance of social connections for human well-being and highlights the psychological influence of shared energy. One well-documented effect of shared energy is emotional contagion.

Emotional contagion in relationships refers to the phenomenon where one partner's emotions and moods can directly influence the other partner. This transmission of emotions occurs through conscious and unconscious channels, including verbal communication, body language, facial expressions, and physiological responses.

Emotional contagion can significantly impact the partnership's emotional climate and overall dynamic. Positive emotions such as happiness, excitement, and affection can enhance mutual well-being and a supportive environment. Conversely, negative emotions such as stress, anger, and sadness can propagate tension, conflict, and emotional distress, leading to cycles of negative interactions.

In your relationship, you must be consciously aware of your actions and behaviors and their impact on your relationship. A single compassionate act can create a domino effect that vibrates through the fibers of your relationship, elevating the vibrational frequency of your entire union, or a negative act and lowering the vibrational frequency. Now, imagine what two or three conscious and compassionate acts could do. How would this elevate the state of the vibrational frequency of your relationship every day, unifying your oneness?

∞∞∞

Another aspect of this universal law is the appreciation of your diversity. Appreciating the beauty of diversity within your relationship is paramount. Recognizing that both you and your partner are uniquely diverse through your cultures, beliefs, experiences, backgrounds, and talents helps enrich your relationship's collective creativity. Rather than viewing these differences as challenges, you must acknowledge and celebrate your differences, enhancing the divinely shaped masterpiece you create together.

Your relationship expands and becomes more prosperous as you and your partner acknowledge and appreciate your differences as positive attributes. These differences can encompass various aspects such as financial habits, spirituality, child-rearing, displays of affection, leadership, and communication abilities. Accepting who they are reflects your capacity to value them, and vice versa. Instead of feeling compelled to change or alter your partner, nurture the many differences that make your relationship unique and wondrous while connecting as one.

Consider the story of Milton and Glory, a couple facing a period of emotional distance. Instead of retreating into individual struggles, they consciously aligned the vision they shared for their relationship through carefully chosen words, actions, and reactions. They were able to create a safe space for effectively communicating their differences of opinion and overcoming challenges together. They established a sense of interconnectedness, transforming their challenges into a catalyst for deeper intimacy and growth through open communication and shared practices.

∞∞∞

Living in alignment with the Law of Divine Oneness involves developing conscious connectedness. Mindfulness becomes necessary as you recognize the impact of your thoughts and actions on your life and relationship. It doesn't matter if it's feelings of resentment, past challenges, negative responses, or an intention for relational harmony; each act becomes a deliberate contributor to the foundational layers of your relationship. Therefore, you must be aware and mindful of your thoughts, feelings, and actions. Which are either strengthening or breaking down your relationship's foundational layers.

The first foundational layer is how you think and feel about yourself. The hustle and bustle of our outer world often directs our lives, making us forget how to think, feel, and speak oneness within ourselves. Therefore, you must realize that the first and most important relationship in the universe is the one you have with yourself. If you are not loving, harmonious, and gracious with yourself, how can you expect those things from your partner?

Deliberately choose thoughts, feelings, and actions that positively contribute to the higher vibrational frequency of your being. Your awareness of universal oneness extends your ability to be forgiving, compassionate, and responsible for the good of yourself and your partner. How can you extend forgiveness and compassion to anyone else if your forgiveness and compassion tanks are empty? It would be best if you filled up your

MANIFEST A JOY-FILLED RELATIONSHIP

tanks to "overflowing" so that you have enough to spare and share.

Like a skilled gardener tending to each plant, removing weeds, and providing essential nutrients, you must cultivate your thoughts, feelings, and actions with mindfulness. Be consciously aware of any negative thoughts, feelings, or actions that can undermine your positive efforts. Focus on nurturing positive seeds, growing healthy plants, and producing rich fruit. Stay vigilant by guarding the gate of your mind and denying access to any unwanted, uninvited, and unproductive guests.

If you believe your actions don't affect your partner or relationship, you hold a perspective that hinders your desires. Aligning your actions and thoughts helps manifest your desires in the physical realm. Imagine a moment in the future when you feel frustrated or angry. Instead of letting these emotions take root and spread, as a conscious practitioner of the Law of Divine Oneness, pause, reflect, and transform negative energy into a positive force. Doing so uplifts your vibrational frequency and positively impacts your relationship. This practice helps you become aware and gain control over your inner world and manifest your desired outcomes in your outer world.

∞∞∞

Here are some journaling prompts to help you shift your perspective and encourage self-reflection. Use these as a starting point and create additional prompts that can assist you in building awareness.

Consciousness Building Journaling Prompts

- ❖ Write down all the ways you love and support yourself. Then, reflect on ways you could enhance and strengthen your self-love. How can you improve your self-love, and how will it show up in your relationship? Note: Selfishness, conceit, narcissism, arrogance, entitlement, and vanity, to name a few, are not what is meant by self-love.

- ❖ Reflect on a recent interaction with your partner where you felt a strong connection. What aspects of that interaction highlighted the concept of oneness for you?

- ❖ Consider a challenge or disagreement you've faced in your relationship. How might viewing the situation through the lens of oneness change your perspective or approach?

- ❖ Describe a time when you and your partner shared a moment of profound understanding or empathy. How did this experience develop your sense of unity?

- ❖ Think about the qualities or traits you admire in your partner. How do these qualities reflect the interconnected nature of your relationship?

- ❖ Explore a shared goal or aspiration you have with your partner. How does working towards this goal together strengthen your bond and reinforce your sense of oneness?

- Reflect on a past conflict or misunderstanding with your partner. How might recognizing your shared interconnectedness have influenced the outcome or resolution?

- Imagine your relationship as a beautiful picture made up of all your shared experiences. What common themes or patterns do you notice when you think about how these experiences are connected?

- Consider the concept of emotional contagion – the idea that emotions can be transferred between individuals. How does this phenomenon manifest in your relationship and contribute to your sense of unity?

- Explore moments of synchronicity or serendipity in your relationship – times when events seemed to align effortlessly. What do these moments reveal about the interconnected nature of your partnership?

- Imagine your relationship as a garden of consciousness that requires monitoring, patience, and dedication. What practices or actions can you incorporate into your daily life to tend to this garden and strengthen your sense of oneness with your partner? What will bear healthy, loving fruit? What weed-like things do you need to discard?

- We encourage you to engage in open and honest dialogue about understanding oneness and how it manifests in your relationship. This could involve discussing shared values, goals, aspirations, and the challenges you face. What could you change to enhance oneness, and how would those things influence the overall temperament of your relationship?

If this concept of journaling seems scary, tedious, a waste of time, or like a useless diary, we encourage you to try it anyway. Be willing to try something new. Try journaling individually or collectively for a week. Journaling has known benefits such as enhancing self-awareness, reducing stress, promoting emotional clarity, supporting achievements, improving problem-solving skills, conscious oneness, and more. Developing the awareness that we are all one and energetically connected is not a weakness but a strength.

∞∞∞

Partners who align their aspirations and work towards shared goals embody the Law of Divine Oneness. Your collective energy propels you forward, creating a sense of unity and purpose that transcends your individual ambitions.

Unity in your relationship refers to recognizing and cultivating the inherent bond between you and your partner.

Imagine a couple engaged in a heartfelt conversation. Partner A expresses joy, and Partner B responds with genuine warmth. The positive energy resonates between them, creating a loving exchange. Conversely, if Partner B is tense, distant, or uninterested, Partner A may feel the energetic shift, illustrating the interconnected nature of emotional states. Being present and aware helps you reign in your focus and share in your partner's joy and enthusiasm, creating emotional connections instead of discord.

Instead of viewing your relationship as two separate entities coming together, embrace the idea that you are already unified at a fundamental level. This shift in perspective fosters a sense of shared purpose, mutual support, and unconditional love. When you and your partner recognize your genuine connection, you can approach challenges as a united front, strengthening the foundation of your relationship and building resiliency. This connection takes time and intentionality. Therefore, every thought, action, and emotion must align with your desired connection for your relationship. Allowing for negative thoughts, actions, or feelings of any caliber can reset and wipe out any progress you may have made. Do not be discouraged; stay steadfast and hold the vision of your relationship in the forefront of your mind, bringing constant and conscious awareness to the thoughts, feelings, and actions you choose. Ask yourself, "Is this thought, feeling, or action one that builds or destroys our connection?

Consider emotional reactions to challenges that prompt one partner to make decisions independently of the other. Recognize that these reactions are not separate inconsequential events but threads intricately woven into your shared experiences. Like threads, choices alter the fabric's texture and color, influencing the relationship's overall pattern. Seeking your partner's opinion in relationship decisions is just one piece of a multi-faceted garment. Ultimately, the choices you make determine the appearance and quality of the finished product. But the good news is you can change the appearance as you move forward.

Note that your past experiences and decisions, good, bad, or indifferent, must remain in the past, and you must form new habits and choices. Your ability to manifest a relationship that reflects your desires requires that you till the soil and plant new seeds, being ever-so-forgiving of last year's unproductive harvest - if necessary.

Picture a couple experiencing a shared moment of joy or sorrow. The Law of Divine Oneness manifests as an emotional bridge connecting their hearts. In moments of shared happiness, the tone is similar to the shared joy, while shared sorrows create an empathetic duo. Genuinely sharing in your partner's joy or sorrow allows you to emit emotional energy shared between you and your partner that will build connecting emotional bridges for closeness and intimacy. This adds to emotional deposits into your relationship bank account, offsetting times when you encounter emergency emotional withdrawals - subsequently lessening the chances of possible emotional overdrafts that could leave your relationship depleted. Being emotionally available when your partner needs it builds oneness.

Consider Irving and Mia, a couple navigating a period of heightened stress. By remembering the principles within the Law of Divine Oneness, they consciously reframed their challenges as shared experiences rather than individual burdens. This shift in perspective allowed them to lean on each other, conquer the problem together, and transform their connection into a source of strength amidst adversity. By aligning their oneness, they began meditating together for a deeper connection, journaling for an outlet to review their part in past and current issues, and taking daily walks together to relieve stress and an opportunity to talk.

∞∞∞

Acknowledging the interconnected nature of your relationship encourages empathy and compassion within your bond. When you recognize that you are a grave part of the whole, you become more attuned to each other's needs, emotions, and life experiences. Attunement improves your bond and supports a sense of oneness.

Viewing your relationship through the window of oneness promotes collaborative problem-solving. Instead of approaching conflicts from a place of individual interests, you work together to find solutions that benefit the relationship. Teamwork increases effective communication, mutual respect, synchronization, and gratitude.

The Law of Divine Oneness cultivates gratitude within your relationship. When you acknowledge the interconnectedness of all things, you become more appreciative of the love, support, and joy you receive from each other. This gratitude develops a positive, supportive dynamic. You don't have to look for things to be grateful for; the law attracts them to you as you become centered in gratitude.

∞∞∞

Exercises and activities to develop a sense of oneness in your relationship are included to help you transition from theory to practice. Each exercise requires vulnerability and a willingness to be open and honest. By honoring your shared journey to a healthy relationship, you can reinforce your bond and create an atmosphere of love, trust, and respect - right from where you are.

Mindfulness practices play a crucial role in your relationship journey. Meditation, for instance, helps you become more in sync with the present moment and the joined nature of your thoughts and emotions. Mindful communication exercises further enhance the awareness of the impact of words and expressions on your relational dynamic.

Transformative dialogue techniques, from active listening to empathetic communication, you gain skills to elevate your awareness and conversations, encouraging the creation of a safe space of openness.

Lastly, you can incorporate these actionable steps and practices inspired by the first law into your daily life. From shared meditations to acts of kindness, these practices become the building blocks of a love that deepens over time, creating a reservoir of shared experiences and joy - a reservoir that enriches and enhances your relationship with a love that extends beyond the confines of individual egos.

Practical Insight: We encourage you to choose the easiest and most comfortable practice and gradually explore them all. Remember, this is a journey, so take your time to discover the best practices for you. There is no "one-size fits all!"

Connection Building Practices/Techniques/Exercises

- ❖ Engage in activities together with full awareness. Whether sharing a meal or conversing, be present in the moment. This practice promotes a more profound sense of connection by acknowledging the shared space you inhabit. More than being in the same space is required. You must intentionally be present and attentive, offering your undivided attention whenever you engage in activities together. Both partners must turn off or silence all electronic devices only to be answered for emergencies. When engaging in activities to strengthen being present, start with doing something small that requires fifteen minutes or less if this is an underdeveloped area in your relationship.

- ❖ Create a vision board together, visualizing shared dreams and aspirations. This collaborative act aligns your energies towards a common purpose, enhancing your shared journey. It allows you to create dreams together that encompass both partners' views, desires, and perspectives while collectively working on any areas that may not be in alignment. This activity can be done together or during separate times, allowing couples to come together later and elaborate on their posted visions for the future and the relationship.

- ❖ Sit in a comfortable position facing each other. Consciously release all thoughts of negativity, blame, or resentment. Take deep breaths and visualize a glowing thread or stream connecting your hearts. Inhale shared positive or radiant energy; release any tensions or concerns as you exhale. This exercise promotes a sense of universal energy and connection. One partner can practice this exercise first by themselves to become open before inviting their partner to join, especially if there's currently a lower frequency of shared energy between you. Initially, you might find this difficult, but stay with it.

- ❖ Maintain a journal together, expressing gratitude for daily moments, both mundane and extraordinary. This practice highlights the awareness of shared experiences, brings awareness to the importance of gratefulness, and reinforces the interconnected nature of your journey together. You decide whether to share the entries or save them for later. If you choose to read the entries, refrain from commenting negatively. If you decide to discuss them later at the end of the week (month), pick a place and time to share without distractions to reinforce gratitude and build connections openly. The key point is to keep an open mind and not expect more from yourself or your partner; growth takes time. Take baby steps to keep the process flowing. Enjoy the process and keep working on gratitude to shift your perspective from problems to the future's positive possibilities.

- ❖ Practice meditation and visualization techniques that develop a shared space of oneness. Visualize areas of your relationship that need nurturing. This practice connects you to the universe, creating unity and strengthening your emotional bonds. It also opens up the channels for other universal laws to work together.

❖ Create practices of connection that reinforce the idea of oneness, joy, and love within your relationship. Practices could include daily check-ins (texts, emails, or phone calls), gratitude exercises (love notes, text of gratitude, or words of encouragement), or shared activities (cooking, bathing, chores, nightly bed talks) that celebrate and encourage your willingness to connect differently.

These practices are designed to help you stay connected and aligned with each other's needs and desires on a daily basis. Avoid feelings of anger, resentment, or disappointment if it takes you or your partner time to develop these new habits. Stay positive in supporting each other's efforts, even if it starts one-sided. Start small, initially one day a week. Then, work your way up to two days, and so forth, until you have collectively agreed and established habits of connection that work in your relationship.

Speak – Repeat Exercise

Active listening activities are instrumental in developing oneness. Active listening involves fully concentrating, understanding, responding, and remembering the other person's words. Reflective dialogue takes this further by having partners reflect back on what they heard to ensure understanding and empathy.

Choose a quiet, comfortable setting free from distractions, ensuring that both partners are in a relaxed state of mind.

THE LAW OF ONENESS

Speaker Role: One partner (the speaker) talks about a specific topic or shares their feelings regarding one particular item for 1-2 minutes without interruption. They should focus on expressing their emotions and thoughts clearly without anger, hostility, or accusation. Stay with only one topic at a time. Staying within the allotted time frame is essential.

Listener Role: The other partner (the listener) pays close attention without interruptions. After the speaker finishes, the listener reflects on what they heard. For example, "What I hear you saying is that you feel [emotion] because [reason]. Did I get that right?"

If the speaker feels the listener didn't quite capture their message, they can clarify, and the listener tries again until the speaker feels understood.

The listening partner validates the speaker's feelings, even if they don't entirely agree. For example, "It makes sense that you feel [emotion] given [situation]. I can see why you would feel that way."

Validation doesn't mean agreeing but acknowledging the speaker's feelings as legitimate. You are trying to get an understanding, and the way to understand is by thoroughly listening and comprehending.

After the speaker feels heard and validated, switch roles. The listener now becomes the speaker and vice versa, repeating the process.

Benefits: Enhances understanding and empathy between partners.

Reduces misunderstandings and promotes emotional safety.

Builds trust and strengthens the relationship.

The Gottman Method - Love Maps and Open-Ended Questions

Technique: Dr. John Gottman's "Love Maps" concept involves knowing your partner's inner world through open-ended questions. This method helps partners stay connected by helping them understand each other's thoughts, feelings, and experiences on a deeper level.

Love Map Building Exercise

Prepare Questions - Use a list of open-ended questions designed to explore each other's inner worlds and reconnect with the person you are now.

Examples (You can change each example to fit your relationship or create your own open-ended questions):

"What are some of your current life dreams and aspirations?"

"Who has been a positive influence in your life recently and why?"

"What are some of your favorite ways to relax?"

"Can you tell me about a challenge you're currently facing and how it makes you feel?"

You can try our recommended board game for couples called Better Topics. Visit their website to purchase and get more information at www.bettertopics.com

One partner asks a question and listens attentively while the other answers. It's important to listen without interrupting or judging.

After the partner answers, the questioner can ask follow-up questions to deepen the conversation. For instance, "What about that dream excites you the most?" or "How did that influence or shape your perspective?"

Show genuine interest and appreciation for the partner's responses. You can say things like, "I didn't know that about you, thank you for sharing," or "I really appreciate you opening up about that."

After a few questions, switch roles so that both partners have the opportunity to ask and answer questions.

Benefits

- ❖ It deepens mutual understanding, emotional connection, and builds gratitude.

- ❖ It encourages open communication and curiosity about each other.

- ❖ It strengthens the sense of partnership and intimacy.

Gratitude and Shared Joy Exercise

Engaging in positive activities together and sharing gratitude can significantly enhance feelings of closeness and appreciation within a relationship.

Each day, set aside 5-10 minutes to share three things you are grateful for in your partner.

Focus on specific actions or qualities. For example, "I'm grateful for how you made dinner tonight; it made me feel cared for," rather than a generic "Thank you for everything."

Joyful Activities Exercise

Select activities both you and your partner enjoy. Activities could include walking in the park, cooking a meal together, trying a new hobby, or having a movie night. Decide which activities you will do beforehand. Don't underestimate the joy and connection that doing little things together can bring.

Schedule regular events. Commit to regularly engaging in your chosen activities on the proposed day and time. Make sure you keep your commitment to yourself, your partner, and your relationship.

During and after your activities, take time to talk about what you enjoyed. For example, "I loved how we laughed so much during our hike today; it felt really good to connect with you."

Remember to express gratitude. Thank each other for the experience. For instance, "Thank you for planning this date; it was really fun."

Weekly Reflection Exercise

At the end of each week, reflect on the positive moments shared and express gratitude for these experiences. Discuss what made these moments special and how they strengthened your connection.

Based on these reflections, plan future activities that can bring similar joy and connection.

Benefits

- ❖ It reinforces positive feelings and mutual appreciation.

- ❖ Creates a reservoir of happy memories that strengthen the relationship.

- ❖ It enhances the emotional bond through shared experiences and gratitude.

Love Techniques and Exercises

Connecting deeply with your partner to obtain universal oneness involves your willingness to engage in spiritual and emotional practices that bring you closer together. Below are three love techniques and exercises designed to enrich your relationship by drawing upon this wonderous, almost mystical source of unity and affection.

Heart Coherence Meditation for Couples Exercise

Heart coherence meditation focuses on aligning the heart's rhythms with positive emotions, promoting a deep sense of connection and well-being. This technique helps you synchronize your heartbeats and energy, creating a unified emotional and spiritual bond.

Choose a quiet, comfortable space where you won't be disturbed. If desired, dim the lights and create a calming atmosphere with soft music or nature sounds.

Sit comfortably facing each other, close enough to hold hands or touch gently. Ensure both partners are relaxed and open.

Close your eyes and take a few deep breaths together, inhaling deeply through the nose and exhaling slowly through the mouth.

Once you are both relaxed, place your hand on your heart and focus on your heartbeat.

Begin to synchronize your breathing with your partner. Inhale together for a count of four, hold for four, and exhale for four. Continue this pattern, feeling the rhythm of your partner's breath.

As you continue to breathe together, focus on generating positive emotions such as love, appreciation, and gratitude. Visualize these feelings emanating from your heart center.

Imagine a warm, glowing light of love and positive energy flowing from your heart to your partner's heart with each breath. Feel this energy connecting and intertwining, creating a powerful bond.

Continue this meditation for 10-15 minutes, maintaining the focus on your heart connection and the shared positive energy.

After the meditation, take a moment to reflect on the experience. Open your eyes, and share your feelings and sensations with each other.

Benefits

- ❖ It promotes emotional and spiritual synchronization.

- ❖ It enhances empathy, compassion, and deep emotional connection.

- ❖ Reduces stress and develops a sense of unity and peace.

Sacred Touch Ritual for Couples Exercise

The sacred touch ritual involves intentional, mindful physical touch infused with love and reverence. This practice helps couples connect on a deeper, more intimate level, tapping into the sacred aspect of their relationship.

Create a comfortable, serene space with soft lighting, candles, and calming music. Make the area inviting with pillows and blankets.

Sit facing each other and set a mutual intention for the ritual. This could be to deepen your connection, express love, or simply to be present with each other.

Spend a few minutes breathing deeply together, inhaling, and exhaling in unison to create a sense of harmony.

Gently touch each other's hands, mindfully exploring the sensation. Focus on being present and feeling the connection through your touch.

Gradually move to other areas, such as the arms, shoulders, and face, maintaining a slow, intentional pace. Use gentle strokes, caresses, and light pressure to convey love and care.

Allow your touch to communicate your feelings. Focus on expressing love, appreciation, and reverence through each touch. Pay attention to your partner's responses and adjust accordingly.

Conclude the ritual with a long, heartfelt embrace. Feel the warmth and energy of your partner's body and allow yourselves to melt into the connection.

After the ritual, take a moment to share your experiences and feelings. Discuss what you enjoyed and how the sacred touch affected you.

Benefits

- ❖ It enhances physical intimacy and emotional closeness.

- ❖ It promotes a sense of reverence and sacredness in the relationship.

- ❖ It deepens mutual appreciation and love.

Soul-Gazing for Couples Exercise

Soul-gazing involves maintaining deep, uninterrupted eye contact with your partner, allowing you to connect on a soul level. This practice helps partners see and feel each other's true essence, fostering profound intimacy and unity.

Find a quiet, comfortable space where you can sit facing each other without distractions. Dim the lights and create a peaceful atmosphere.

Sit comfortably close to each other, ensuring your knees are touching or almost touching. Hold hands if it feels natural.

Start by closing your eyes and taking a few deep breaths together to relax and center yourselves.

Open your eyes and look into each other's eyes. Focus on one eye (it's easier than trying to focus on both). Maintain a soft, relaxed gaze without straining.

Continue gazing into each other's eyes for 3-5 minutes. If you feel the urge to look away or giggle, acknowledge it and gently return your focus.

As you gaze, try to see beyond the physical appearance and connect with your partner's essence. Feel the love and energy flowing between you.

Notice any emotions that arise during the exercise. Allow yourself to feel and acknowledge these emotions without judgment.

Share a warm, heartfelt embrace after the exercise. Feel the connection you've established and hold onto that sense of unity.

Take a moment to discuss the exercise. Share what you felt, any emotions that came up, and how the experience impacted you.

Benefits

- ❖ It deepens emotional and spiritual intimacy.

- ❖ It enhances mutual understanding and empathy.

- ❖ It improves connection and oneness.

You have set the stage for a relationship rooted in mindfulness, collaboration, and shared growth. In the subsequent chapters, you will build upon this, exploring vibrational energies, the correspondence between internal and external realities, and the transformative power of intentional action.

Your journey to a joy-filled relationship continues as the cosmic principles guide you toward a more enlightened and connected union, and your love becomes etched in the stars. Deep desires become true possibilities by learning and applying universal laws in all areas of your life.

In *What We Believe* by Don Nedd and commentary by Helen W. Carry (1990, p. 7), the concept of love is eloquently expressed: "Love is the idea in Divine Mind of universal oneness that attracts, binds, cements, harmonizes everything in God's universe. Can you imagine how beautiful all our lives would be if everyone based his thinking on Love ..."

Chapter Two
THE LAW OF VIBRATION
Understanding the Energetic Frequency in Relationships

In the Law of Vibration, you explore energetic frequencies, recognizing that everything in the universe is in motion, vibrating at its own unique frequency. This law is the basis for understanding how your thoughts, feelings, and state of being contribute to the vibrational energy you emit. When applied to your relationship, it suggests that you emanate specific energetic vibrations, influencing your overall relational atmosphere.

You become what you think about most of the time; your relationship is no different. Your relationship doesn't become what you want or desire but what you form through your vibrational energy of thoughts and feelings.

Consider the significance created within a relationship when a couple shares a common goal or vision; the collective energy generated becomes a powerful force that influences the outcomes they collectively experience.

Tina's Account

I remember going through a similar situation where we created a common goal or vision for our family. It was during the early years of our marriage, and we had lived in our home for less than a year. With two kids under four and Jason's mom living with us, Jason started feeling stuck and unhappy in his job. Our evening conversations after work revolved around the same topic night after night. Jason began to dread going to work and often talked about leaving. However, he enjoyed his clients and had a good rapport with them. He loved what he did, just not who he did it for.

One evening, during our usual conversation, I suggested he quit and start his own business. He looked at me with wide eyes and said, "Quit?" I replied, "Yes, quit. If you can do it for someone else, you can do it for yourself!" After a moment of silence and looking down at the floor, he turned to me and detailed all the reasons why he couldn't. As I responded, I began to paint a picture for him of running his own business, interacting with happy clients, and earning enough to match and exceed his current salary. He bought into the vision and said, "Let's do it!" I reassured him that I would continue working and do whatever was necessary to ensure we were okay.

Over the next week, we devised a plan and set a common goal. Jason quit his job, and we stepped out on faith. It has been over 27 years, and we never looked back! Because we shared the same vision, it became a powerful force that influenced the outcome of our collective experience.

This chapter lays the groundwork for a revealing exploration of your relationship's vibrational dimensions. We are equipping you with the knowledge and tools to consciously shape the energetic frequencies within your intimate connections and change them forever.

This law proposes that energy makes up everything in the universe. Each atom, cell, and thought releases its own unique frequency. When you align those frequencies with your intentions and goals, you harmonize your vibrations with your desired energies. Studies in psychophysiology and bioenergetics provide a lens through which you can comprehend the energetic vibes in your relationship. Science tells us that everyone gives off measurable electric fields that are affected by their emotions. In addition, research studies on heart rate variability show how emotional health is linked to physical well-being, confirming how vibrations directly affect life and relationships.

Let's go even further and examine the realm of quantum physics. This concludes that even objects that appear solid are, at their core, comprised of vibrating particles. This means that nothing, no matter the appearance, is solid. Each object simultaneously vibrates at a specific frequency, adding to the universe's overall energetic harmony.

Physicists contend that everything you see has been put together, or is being held together, by your thoughts. Can you grasp that concept? Your thoughts give you the ability to influence and alter anything in the universe through your mental frequency. Are you ready to become an intentional influencer?

You might be wondering what that has to do with your relationship. Everything!

Supported by undeniable data, this belief proves that your thoughts shape and reshape your world, including your relationship. Did you get that? Your thoughts, not your partner's, your boss', your children's, or your parents', but your thoughts can reshape your relationship. How powerful is that? How powerful are you?

We realize this might be news to some and a friendly reminder to others. Nevertheless, we pose this question to all: Have you ever paused to consider, before you think those thoughts and utter those unkind words, what kind of impact they will have on your relational landscape? It doesn't matter what relationship – are you stopping to choose thoughts and words that align with the positive frequencies of the universe? Truly grasping the power you possess should discourage you from merely thinking and speaking without intentionality.

If you remember nothing else from this book, please remember that you shape and create the relationship you desire through the power of your thinking. It is not done through force, wanting to control others, or by some mere chance. But you influence your outer world by desiring, thinking, and aligning with positive vibrations. So, are you ready to take back your power and create or recreate the relationship you truly want instead of the one you unconsciously allowed to manifest?

∞∞∞

At the heart of this law lies the realization that your thoughts, emotions, and actions send out vibrational frequencies. Everyone is a symphony of frequencies, influenced by their thoughts, feelings, beliefs, experiences, and overall well-being. Understanding your own frequencies is the first step toward aligning them with your partner's. The law encourages you to become conscious choreographers of your shared energetic frequencies that shape your connection.

These frequencies influence the vibrations in and around your relationship. These vibrations exist whether you acknowledge them or not. Therefore, when you set clear and positive intentions, you attune yourself to harmonious vibrational currents. In contrast, when you fail to set clear, positive intentions, you attune yourself and your relationship to uncertainty.

It is vital to identify your personal and relational vibrational energies. Vibrational energies refer to the energetic frequencies that you and your partner release and interact with on a daily basis. The unseen but evident essence influences the quality of your interactions, communication, and overall accord in your relationship. Every thought, emotion, and action carries a specific vibration that contributes to the energetic feel of your partnership.

Both partners must examine their collective vibrational frequencies objectively to fully comprehend their individual frequencies. Your emotional tones, communication patterns, and shared experiences all impact your overall vibrational environment.

Enhancing self-awareness allows you to recognize your vibrational patterns and understand the energies they bring into your relationship. Techniques like biofeedback and heart coherence exercises enable you to deeply tune into your energetic frequencies.

Through the practice of simple techniques for raising your vibrations and learning to align them creatively within the relational space, you establish connections that can turn your partnership into a beautiful and sustainable adventure with everlasting love, joy, happiness, and gratitude.

How do we know? Because we have done it and are still doing it! Despite challenges that could have caused us to walk away and throw in the towel when things seemed bleak and irreconcilable. It took us to turn within and find what we needed to change to change our relationship, not our partner.

You are a collection of frequencies, an energetic signature that emanates from your core. Understanding your frequencies is an essential step toward aligning them with the harmonious structure of your relationship.

Take moments for self-reflection to tune into your energetic frequency. What emotions control your inner being? How do your thoughts influence your vibration? By developing awareness, you can consciously shape and enhance your frequencies.

∞∞∞

A positive mindset continuously emits higher vibrational frequencies. Cultivating gratitude, optimism, and mindfulness elevates your vibrations, creating a magnetic energy that influences you and the relationship.

Every positive thought and act of kindness initiates a domino effect within the ocean of vibrations. Just as every negative thought or act of selfishness will also initiate a corresponding domino effect. The Law of Vibration illustrates that those vibrations will extend far beyond their immediate surroundings, impacting the connecting fibers of your joined existence. Like a pebble tossed into a pond, positive vibrations will expand outward. This expansion has the power to uplift or discourage the collective energy of your relationship and the universe. Everyone possesses the power to contribute to the nature of the universal strain, highlighting the interconnected nature of all things.

However, the law guides and directs each partner's energies and the collective vibrations that define your relational essence. Every positive and negative vibration impacts your relationship. You and your partner's interactions form and shape this unique relational vibration.

Realizing that your relationship's vibrational frequency is co-created is important. You and your partner contribute to it through your shared experiences, communication styles, actions, beliefs, and culture. Those vibrations and frequencies will either impact your relationship positively or negatively. That means that your shared interactions vibrate out and may return back as blame, arguments, finger-pointing, unaccountability, suppressed emotions, invalidation, immaturity, and an unwillingness to change. Or they can show up as acceptance, support, accountability, cooperation, emotional intelligence, and empathy.

For instance, during conflicts, your emotions release distinct vibrations. By approaching conflict resolution with a focus on raising your vibrational frequency, you and your partner can transform your old ways of handling conflict into new habits that add value and foundational depth creating a more positive relational vibration.

Awareness of your energetic emissions and consciously choosing positive vibrations will promote self-growth and enhance your relational character. Nevertheless, actively and consciously engaging in positive relational co-creation adopts a sense of shared responsibility. The insight must come from your awareness that the choice is yours in building and creating the relationship you desire. When you intentionally choose positive thoughts, feelings, words, actions, and reactions to create positive vibrations, you individually and collectively contribute to a supportive and fulfilling relationship dynamic. Whereas, negative energies, separately or collectively, whether intentional or unintentional, can disrupt this harmony, creating discord and tension within your relationship.

As you learn to tune into your vibrational energies, you make shifts to harmonize and establish unbreakable connections. Techniques inspired by positive psychology and energy healing modalities become valuable allies in aligning your energies and strengthening connections.

Shared story

Eddie and Christina were constantly arguing because of Eddie's untidiness. Despite being married for over 18 years, neither was willing to understand the other's point of view during arguments. Eddie tried to justify his actions by reminding Christina that he had warned her before they had gotten married. He even hired outside help to resolve the issue, but Christina felt it hadn't resolved anything. Christina defended her stance by explaining how she always felt judged when guests visited. Feeling unappreciated and ignored, her anger grew into resentment. It wasn't until Christina started practicing heart-mind coherence that she began to appreciate Eddie for his positive qualities and traits. She realized her frustration was due to being out of balance with chores, work, and self-care. She began focusing on what was going right in their relationship rather than what was going wrong. This shift in perspective and new awareness made her more receptive to other solutions instead of complaining about Eddie's seeming flaws. Through empathy, changing perspective, and adding self-care regiments, she was able to propose a solution that benefited both her and Eddie.

Heart-mind coherence refers to a state of alignment and harmony between your heart and mind. This state occurs when your emotions, thoughts, and physiological responses are synchronized, leading to improved emotional stability, mental clarity, and overall well-being. It is often achieved through mindfulness, meditation, and heart-focused breathing, promoting a balanced connection between your emotional and cognitive functions.

Consider for a moment you envision a future abundant with joy and all good things. By focusing on establishing a desired outcome, you consciously create a higher frequency through the Law of Vibration. This vibrational suggestion attracts similar frequencies, aligning opportunities and experiences with your held intentions.

Now, apply this to your relationship. Envision your relationship as fulfilling and happy, your mindset vibrating higher intentional energy through the Law of Vibration. This energy initiates being open, optimistic, and receptive to forming meaningful connections with your partner, irrespective of your past. Your thoughts, emotions, and intentions send out energies that positively influence the dynamics you have with your partner. By aligning your intentions with your actions and thoughts, you attract balanced and matching experiences within your relationship.

You release emotions into the vibrational realm by focusing on negative thoughts about your partner or relationship, such as fear, doubt, resentment, or unhappiness. As your mind continually rehearses these negative thoughts, your energy vibrates at a lower frequency, affecting your physical and emotional health and validating those negative beliefs. In contrast, when you release positive emotions like love, joy, gratitude, and compassion, your energy rises to a higher vibrational frequency. These positive energies enhance your personal experiences and resonate outward, positively impacting your partner and relationship in the physical realm.

Understanding how you are vibrationally sending out what you don't want and receiving more of it is the first step in using this law to create the relationship you truly desire through conscious vibrations.

∞∞∞

As you build on your foundational understanding, know that there are practical techniques that can raise and align your vibrational energies. Any mindfulness practices, such as meditation and conscious breathing, serve as powerful tools to help you strengthen emotional coherence and raise vibrations.

Just as music can evoke emotions, the energetic frequencies in your relationship carry emotional notes. A shared laugh, a comforting touch, or a supportive gesture contributes to the notes of emotional worth. Remember to appreciate the power that little things can have on your connections. Making your partner feel valued and appreciated in conflicting or stressful times can have immeasurable and immediate effects on rebuilding and strengthening emotional connection and raising your overall relational vibrations.

A comforting touch signals to your partner that you understand and validate their feelings at that moment. Valuing your partner, regardless of the situation causing them discomfort, reassures your partner of their worth to you. This action doesn't signify that your partner is right or wrong but that you recognize and support them.

Incorporating intentional practices into your relationship routine amplifies the vibrational quality. Expressing gratitude, engaging in acts of kindness, and unwavering support contribute to a higher vibrational frequency.

"The highest state of love is not a relationship, it's a state of being." - Eckhart Tolle.

Eckhart Tolle's insight encourages you to rise above your current view of your relationship and enter into a state of being where vibrational harmony becomes the natural expression of your connection.

∞∞∞

Aligning with the Law of Vibration starts with being aware of your thoughts and feelings. When you become conscious of your thoughts and feelings, you can change the energy you're vibrating. This awareness forms the basis for improving the energy in your relationship. You can only change something if you're aware it needs changing. Recognizing what needs to change requires both awareness and honesty within yourself.

Recognizing what needs to change does not mean pointing out your partner's imperfections, according to you. All change begins and ends with you. You are working on you, not your partner. Let's take some advice from Michael Jackson and start with the man in the mirror! Each person must put in their work and come to their own realization of what they are thinking and feeling that is not beneficial to their relationship or in alignment with their desires.

Let's consider the analogy of listening to your favorite song at a live concert, where each instrument produces a distinct sound that, when combined, creates a harmonious composition. Now, consider each instrument playing a different song, sound, or vibration that does not mesh well. This misalignment will continue until each instrument finds and corrects its own attunement.

Similarly, individual vibrations may differ within relationships, but they can harmonize with conscious and intentional work to create a unified and beautiful melody.

Mindfulness practices and techniques serve as powerful tools to help you strengthen emotional coherence and raise and align vibrations.

Here are techniques you and your partner can use to assess and raise your vibrational energies. These are suggestions, and you can use or omit them depending on your level of comfort.

THE LAW OF VIBRATION

Practices/Techniques/Exercises

Engaging in **self-reflection/awareness** techniques tunes you into your own energetic frequency, shedding light on dominant emotions and the influence of your thoughts. Reflecting on your thoughts, feelings, and behaviors can help identify patterns contributing to lower vibrations. Developing awareness enables deliberate shaping and refinement of your personal frequencies.

Setting intentions for your relationship ensures that you focus on the qualities you wish to cultivate and the experiences you want to create together.

Mutual support techniques require you to actively engage in ways to support and uplift each other, creating a positive feedback loop that reinforces harmonious vibrations within your relationship.

Focus on love as a powerful energy technique crucial in shifting relational paradigms when intentionally integrated into your daily routines. Consciously developing positive vibrational frequencies within the relationship by expressing love, appreciation, and gratitude raises the energetic frequency of the union regularly, creating a magnetic force that attracts more positivity. Actively reflecting on what you love about your partner, relationship, and yourself raises the vibration around those things and allows for more to manifest.

Visualization exercises enable the setting of clear intentions and mental alignment with desired outcomes, enhancing the attraction of experiences resonating with envisioned goals. Establishing a daily routine of expressing gratitude and appreciation promotes positive vibrations through verbal affirmations, love notes, or simple gestures.

Energy-cleansing practices incorporate techniques like burning sage, smudging, sound healing, or meditation to release stagnant or negative energy from your shared space and facilitate harmonization.

Mindfulness practices such as meditation, yoga, or deep breathing exercises help you become more attuned to your inner state, promote inner peace and harmony, and lay a foundation for harmonious connection.

Incorporating **daily positive affirmations** reshapes thought patterns, elevating personal energies and enhancing relational viewpoints or perspectives.

Affirmations are only half the story. You must use **daily denials** to rid yourself of old thinking and circumstances, then fill those empty spaces with affirmations of what you desire.

Choosing **a healthy lifestyle** reduces stress, contributes to overall well-being, and emits higher vibrations.

- ❖ Eating nutritious foods.

- ❖ Exercising regularly.

- ❖ Getting adequate sleep.

Establishing habits like daily check-ins synchronizes energies and enhances relational importance through **mindful connection** practices.

Establishing **routines of connection** harmonizes personal and relational vibrations, enhancing unity through shared morning routines, evening reflections, or mindful moments.

Recognizing **open communication** as an energetic exchange emphasizes spoken words and underlying vibrational frequencies. Conscious and compassionate communication nurtures vibrational alignment in your relationship. This allows you to express your thoughts, feelings, and needs openly and honestly, developing understanding and empathy between you and your partner. Suggestion: Individually try mind-heart coherence practices first to help open up channels of effective and loving communication.

Shared story

Take, for example, Richard and Bobbie, a couple facing the challenges of balancing demanding careers with their personal lives. Through intentional practices such as shared meditation, mindful connection routines, open communication, and setting positive intentions, they learned to navigate the energetic frequencies associated with stress, relationship frustration, and exhaustion. They found renewed energy individually by consciously aligning their vibrations, strengthening their connection as a couple. By incorporating these practices, they were able to reduce or eliminate stress responders and have more time to enjoy their relationship.

∞∞∞

Once you have taken the steps to elevate your vibrational energy, the focus now shifts to aligning those energies with your partner's. This alignment is about creating a synergistic flow of positive energy between you. Communication and vulnerability play a vital role as you openly discuss and share your emotional states, needs, and desires. By sharing your experiences and actively listening to each other, you establish deeper intimate connections and strive towards creating a safe space for sharing, free of judgment and condemnation.

Aligning your vibrational energies involves finding common ground and being able to align your values, goals, and aspirations. Align the fundamental aspects of your life, such as your vision for the future and core beliefs, to create a sense of unity and purpose within your relationship. Align your energies to move into a space of understanding and forgiveness of past and present challenges. This alignment acts as a powerful catalyst for collectively maintaining higher vibrational frequencies.

In The Revealing Word, Charles Fillmore tells us, "Forgiveness really means the giving up of something" (Fillmore 77). He says, "Forgiveness removes the errors of the mind, and bodily harmony results in consonance with divine law" (Fillmore 77). You can look at forgiveness as a unique tool from the universe that aids in your alignment. Forgiveness is your ability to give up for something better. You give up your old ways of negative thinking and feeling peace and harmony.

Forgiveness is not letting the other person off the hook or conferring with the wrongdoing. No, it releases you from the bondage and negative emotions of the experience. That allows you the freedom to put something better in its place. We know from physics principles that two objects cannot occupy the same space simultaneously. Therefore, if you want something better for your relationship, you must be willing to release the objects (things) that are not working.

Gratitude exercises, acts of kindness, and shared mindfulness activities promote positive energy for establishing alignment. Aligning vibrational energies is dynamic and ongoing. It requires continuous effort, empathy, and mutual support.

Practices/Techniques for Aligning Vibrations

Establishing routines of connection synchronizes your personal and relational vibrations. Promoting and developing unity can be done through shared meditation practices in the morning, evening workouts, or love talks sharing your feelings or concerns.

Starting daily routines nurtures positive vibrations, such as expressing gratitude and appreciation, speaking your partner's love language, or recognizing something your partner said or did that made you feel loved and appreciated.

Mindful Breathing Together

- ❖ Engage in synchronized breathing exercises.

- ❖ As you breathe together, visualize a shared energy field forming between you.

- ❖ Let this energy field encircle you to promote a sense of unity and alignment of vibrations.

Energy-Cleansing Rituals

- ❖ Burn incense, sage, oils, candles, or other items to cleanse and align your energies.

- ❖ Create heart coherence rituals where you and your partner can release stagnant energies.

- ❖ Heighten your awareness to promote fresh and harmonious frequencies.

Shared Meditation

- ❖ Meditate together, guided or unguided, with or without music.

- ❖ Visualize a shared energy field to promote oneness and connection.

- ❖ Align your frequencies to forge connections in the invisible and visible planes.

Conscious Communication

- ❖ Recognize communication as an energetic exchange.

- ❖ Pay attention not only to your spoken words but also to the underlying vibrational frequencies they send out.

- ❖ Conscious and compassionate communication raises vibrational alignment.

- ❖ Integrate techniques like active listening and mindful speaking, ensuring your words contribute to the understanding, connection, and harmonious vibrational exchange.

- ❖ Practice empathy. It also serves as a bridge that aligns relational vibrations, allowing you to understand your partner's frequency.

Shared story

David and Lisa had a long-distance relationship that often caused undue strain on their ability to empathize. They decided to navigate the challenges of long-distance by synchronizing their frequencies through intentional practices such as virtual shared meditations, regular check-ins, and shared activities when together. By aligning their energies, they transformed distance into an opportunity to connect deeper, although they were miles apart.

Using the Law of Vibration as a preventative maintenance mechanism permits your relationship to reap tremendous benefits. Very rarely do you emanate loving thoughts and feelings during conflict. Therefore, as you focus on raising your vibrational frequencies first, you transform discord into opportunities for growth and sustainability.

Practical exercises like the following will increase positive energy and raise vibrational frequencies.

- ❖ Collectively, go through visualization techniques where you imagine your shared goals and ideal relationship, focusing on feelings of love, connection, and harmony.

- ❖ Active listening with empathy involves fully focusing on your partner when they are speaking, ensuring that you understand and validate their feelings. This practice helps build connection and understanding in your relationship.

- ❖ Consider making spontaneous gestures of love and appreciation, as well as intentional acts of kindness, to keep the relationship's energy vibrant and alive.

- ❖ Start each day by engaging in gratitude practices or expressing gratitude for one another and for the relationship itself.

❖ A daily practice of keeping a shared gratitude journal of acknowledging and appreciating your blessings raises individual and relational vibrations.

Visualization, empathetic presence, and heartfelt gratitude are conduits for harmonizing your vibrational energies. You create a relational container where love flows freely and authentic connection thrives.

Shared story

Let's look at Alex and LaAisha, a couple with young children navigating the beginning of their busy lives together. They raised and aligned their relational frequencies by incorporating some of the shared practices. These practices became routine and transformed their partnership. Giving them a new perspective on how to work through life's challenges together without destroying their relationship. Through daily practices, they have formed a partnership based on love, respect, and cooperation.

The Law of Vibration points out the significance of implementing mindfulness and intention in shaping your energetic dynamic. Integrating deliberate routines and practices into your relationship can amplify your vibrational frequency and intentionally build a relationship that reflects your desires.

Nevertheless, you must become consciously aware of the influences shaping and impacting your relational environment. Implementing mindfulness means being tuned in to the conditions, people, and experiences that do not match your desired energetic frequencies. Adjusting your surroundings, activities, and network of friends may be necessary until you have successfully established an awareness of your positive and negative energies and how to change them accordingly. Recognizing the power of mindset and positivity is essential to your journey. Practicing a positive outlook produces higher vibrational frequencies.

The Law of Vibration summons you to recognize your role as a conscious participant in building your relationship dynamics. By understanding and aligning yourself with positive vibrational frequencies, you can step into co-creating, shaping the energetic landscape of your life, and positively contributing to your relationship's synergy. Applying this law grants you the power to mold your reality despite previous beliefs. If the law doesn't work for you, it's not the law!

In *What We Believe* by Don Nedd and commentary by Helen W. Carry ©1990, pg5, the concept of who we are in connection to universal/spiritual Laws: "The truth about every man is that we are spiritual beings (the real of us) living in a spiritual world, governed by spiritual laws. These spiritual laws, or principles, are for everyone and we must put them into practice if we would come into "our inheritance". Do you ever doubt that 2 + 2 = 4? No matter what you apply that mathematical principle to, it always works... If not, there is an error on your part, not the principle."

Chapter Three
THE LAW OF INSPIRED ACTION
Bridging Intention and
Manifestation in Relationships

With all the untapped wonders of the universe, the Law of Inspired Action emerges, steering your relational intentions toward tangible outcomes. The Law of Inspired Action shows you how to bridge the gap between intention and manifestation. It emphasizes the transformative power of aligning purposeful intent with decisive, deliberate steps.

While the Law of Vibration sets the stage, the Law of Inspired Action stresses the importance of taking tangible, actionable, inspired steps to achieve your relationship goals. This law states that deliberate, purposeful steps are essential for manifesting your desires and bringing about positive change. It's not just about wanting a great relationship; heck, everyone wants that. It's about the work you are willing to do to make it great by putting forth intentional efforts and working towards common goals. Think of it like this: You can wish for a clean house, but inspired action must guide you to take the necessary steps to make it happen.

What exactly constitutes an inspired step? An inspired step is an action derived from inner knowing - when something deep within calls you to take action, even when it may not initially make sense.

Therefore, as you read this chapter, it is our deepest desire that you clearly understand that it is more than just taking any action; it's about acting from a place of inner knowing and alignment with the universe. Surrendering to guidance as instinct and listening to one's intuition and inspiration, even when it defies logic or conventional wisdom.

Are you ready because your journey is far from over? Grab your shovel and be inspired to take action to dig deeper!

∞∞∞

This law invites you to recognize opportunities, follow your intuition, and conspire with the universe by aligning your actions with your aspirations. You must be willing to take intentional steps to manifest the dreams and desires for your relationship.

The transformative power of intentional steps goes beyond mere actions and simple surface-level decisions. You must consciously engage in inspired action to have guidance on how to tap into the source to align your deep desires and follow intuition. It is through your alignment with inner knowing that you acquire personal and relational growth. This growth comes out of the expansion of your consciousness or awareness. This awareness comes from clarity regarding your true desires, fears, and motivations. It involves being familiar with subtle cues from within and from the dynamics of your relationship itself.

Realize the importance of transforming your inspired thoughts and feelings into concrete actions. Motivated by inspiration, intentional steps create meaningful and lasting changes in your relationship dynamics. You manifest through the transformative power of aligning your actions with inspired intentions.

Trust is a critical element of this law. Despite outer appearances, you must trust yourself in the process of life and the unfoldment of your relationship desires. One of its main requirements is stepping out of your comfort zone and embracing uncertainty, knowing without reservation that the inner guidance you will receive is steering you toward growth and alignment with your true path. Know, concerning your relationship, that trust translates into openness, vulnerability, and motivation to explore new avenues of connection and communication even when it's uncomfortable.

Like many things you do, your actions will have a chain reaction, shaping and bending your relationship's trajectory for years to come. Therefore, instead of passively waiting for things to happen or relying solely on external situations and circumstances, you must take ownership of the role you play in shaping your relationship. Whether from your past actions or the current ones. Taking a proactive approach will require you to intentionally engage in continuous learning, adaptation, and course correction based on feedback from your experiences and inner guidance.

∞∞∞∞

Inspiration lies in the heart of every thriving relationship - a force that ignites passion, encourages empathy, and improves oneness. It sparks creativity, fuels spontaneity, and fills ordinary moments with extraordinary significance. It lies there dormant, waiting to be awakened in moments of shared belief, in the warmth of cuddling, and in the silence of shared space and unspoken affection.

Even with all its glory and promises, it won't force you to take action. On the contrary, inspiration will sit back in eager anticipation, waiting for its opportunity to gently urge you to take action so that it can help you achieve your desired goals. Anxiously holding its breath, hoping you realize that nothing is unattainable; you just have to have the right desire, followed by the right thoughts, echoed in the right words, seasoned with the right feelings, expressed through the right actions, and followed up with the right reactions to achieve it. While love and attraction may ignite a relationship's initial spark, sustained effort and intentional actions fuel its growth, connection, and longevity. It's not just about feeling love and affection; it's about doing things that show you care and want to grow together. Inspiration is like the drive that keeps things exciting and meaningful. It's what makes your partner feel loved, appreciated, and understood by you and vice versa.

∞∞∞

Essentially, the Law of Inspired Action stresses that decisive action is vital for manifesting your desires. It involves aligning your objectives with planned steps that boost your willingness to work toward your goals. In relationships, this law tells you that no matter how badly you want something, no matter how loudly you express it, and regardless of what your friends may say, the only way to initiate change is to take the first step. However, that's not all; the step must result in action, and that action must be directly aligned with your desired outcome. This sets in motion the processes necessary to manifest your individual and shared visions fueled by inspiration.

THE LAW OF INSPIRED ACTION

The psychology of inspiration helps us realize the impact of countless studies on motivation and goal setting that prove invaluable in understanding why we do what we do. Research demonstrates the significance of setting specific, measurable, achievable, relevant, and time-bound (SMART) goals in various aspects of life; why not in your relationship? At the intersection of inspiration and action are studies on the psychology of passion, emphasizing the role of sustained effort in pursuing meaningful objectives. Do you have passion for the objectives of your relationship?

Although inspiration is a powerful force that can awaken passion and motivation in your relationship, its true potential lies in consciously integrating your inspired thoughts into intentional actions. Inspiration is often described as a burst of creativity or motivation that can arise from various sources. Your burst of inspiration can come from setting shared goals, spending quality time together, improving vulnerability, or any number of things. However, while moments of inspiration can evoke deep feelings of love, passion, and connection, inspiration alone is temporary; it fades over time without deliberate action on your part to anchor it in the visible. Therefore, it is crucial to understand that inspiration alone cannot sustain a thriving relationship over time. Your inspiration must be coupled with clear, intentional action for it to last. Therefore, by intertwining your inspiration with purposeful steps, you can turn those mental feelings into tangible expressions of love, commitment, and care. This synergy of shared inspiration and experiences can boost your relationship.

You can make conscious choices and take deliberate actions that align with your aspirations sparked by inspiration.

For example, suppose you feel inspired to strengthen your communication. In that case, purposeful steps may include setting aside dedicated time for meaningful conversation, learning enhanced communication skills, practicing active listening, and expressing thoughts and feelings openly and honestly. Initially, incorporating these things into your relationship might raise instant inspiration. However, the ongoing practices of these actions drive and sustain lasting joy and happiness. Make sure that you are measuring and paying attention to your action barometer. Don't be fooled by complacency as happiness. Your relationship is supposed to be just as thrilling today as when you first got together. And if it's not, start applying some inspired action guided by intuition through the given tools and techniques. Let's strive to thrive! Anyone can exist.

Having purposeful steps will aid you in bridging the gap between inspiration and reality and filling your relationship with substance and depth. Making sure you take decisive steps demonstrates commitment, effort, and a genuine desire to sustain the connection within your relationship. Over time, consistent and intentional actions based on inspiration will shift your perspective, activate change, and contribute to building a solid union of trust, intimacy, mutual respect, and genuine joy. You don't have to fake it; you can create it. It is yours for the making.

∞∞∞

Psychological research offers insights into the dynamics of motivation, goal setting, and passion. These elements play a fundamental role in guiding purposeful actions within your relationship. Through motivation theories, such as Self-

Determination Theory (SDT), we understand how intrinsic motivation is derived from your personal values and aspirations. Goal-setting theories, such as the SMART goals framework, highlight the effectiveness of setting clear and achievable goals. Passion theories, like the Dualistic Model of Passion, explain how harmonious passion can lead to a loving and balanced relationship.

Motivation, derived from within, fuels your actions and decisions in your relationship. According to SDT, when your actions align with your core values and beliefs, you experience intrinsic motivation, which ignites genuine engagement and satisfaction. This inherent motivation helps you stay committed to your partner, even through challenging times, because your actions resonate with your true self.

Setting goals in your relationship provides direction and purpose. The SMART goals framework - specific, measurable, achievable, relevant, and time-bound - ensures that your relationship goals are clear and attainable. By setting and working towards these goals together, you and your partner create a shared vision for your future, enhancing your bond and commitment to each other.

Passion is another key component that drives relationship dynamics. The Dualistic Model of Passion distinguishes between harmonious and obsessive passion. Harmonious passion, which aligns with your values and integrates well with other aspects of your life, promotes a balanced and intimate relationship. It encourages mutual respect, shared interests, and personal growth, strengthening your connection with your partner.

Before we go on, we want you to stop and take a breather. Awaken your senses and be mindful of every word you read. Now, dive into a deeper, more focused reading. Why? Because in your exploration, you have just uncovered a precious gem. It's easy to mistake it for an ordinary rock, but its true value lies within its understanding. Many couples express dissatisfaction over time, longing for the connection, passion, and intimacy they once had but now struggle to reclaim. Can you relate?

Consequently, countless studies have explored the elusive concept of passion in relationships. Everyone craves it, yet few know where to find it. But fear not, for the answer lies within these pages. In the words you just read and the ones to come. Be aware of simplicity. Pay attention to it. These studies are crucial because they show how sustained effort and commitment contribute to long-term satisfaction. What does that mean for you? It means consistently engaging in inspired actions can ignite, accelerate, and maintain passion, advancing emotional depth, intellectual connection, and lasting intimacy.

This book isn't just another collection of lofty promises; it's a practical guide. A practical guide to help you become aware of and use the laws of the universe to manifest your aspirations and desires for your relationship. Subsequently, by incorporating psychological principles of inspiration and action into your relationship, you will identify just how vital motivation, goal-setting, and persistent effort are in developing and preserving your bond. These insights are meant to empower you to approach your relationship with intentionality and purpose, leveraging inspiration as a channel for positive change

THE LAW OF INSPIRED ACTION

and growth. This stresses the necessity of intentional effort in turning inspired visions into specific outcomes.

Understanding and applying these psychological principles can cultivate a more purposeful and satisfying relationship. Harnessing intrinsic motivation ensures that your actions are aligned with your deepest values, making your relationship more authentic and resilient. Setting SMART goals provides a clear path to achieving your shared aspirations, keeping both partners focused and motivated. Supporting harmonious passion enriches your relationship, allowing it to thrive in a balanced and sustainable way.

In essence, motivation, goal setting, and passion are intertwined elements that guide your relationship toward growth and enjoyment. By integrating these principles into your daily interactions and long-term plans, you create a strong foundation for a lasting and meaningful partnership with an eternal flame. Through motivation, you find the drive to nurture your relationship; through goal setting, you chart a course for your shared future; and through passion, you fill your journey with joy and purpose.

As we build upon the concept of inspiration, it should become evident that turning inspired thoughts and feelings into definite action is critical. Inspired intentions encompass the feelings, values, and aspirations that arise from your ideas of inspiration, such as longing for equal emotional intelligence, enhanced effective communication, enjoyable shared experiences, or passion and intimate progression.

Meaningful and lasting changes in your relationship can be established through planned steps, driven by your ideas, and guided by intuition. Once you understand this transformative influence, it can help you align your actions with your motivated plans, leading to positive outcomes in your relationship.

However, this process requires you to become knowledgeable and a willing participant in several aspects, such as being mindful of your inspired intentions. This requires introspection and self-awareness. You must understand the underlying emotions and values driving your inspiration and recognize how they can positively or negatively influence the relationship.

Your intentional steps are simple but strategic. As a couple, you can work towards creating a plan that outlines specific actions supported by your shared values and objectives. This may involve setting joint goals, defining roles and responsibilities, and establishing timelines for successful implementation. This must be a shared venture where both partners are involved in the planning. Not one assigning the goals, roles, and duties of both partners. It's a total collaboration that requires the active participation of each partner. This supports the value, appreciation, and desires of each partner being considered.

And lastly, your ability to continually develop your relationship relies on the ability to alter your intentions through consistent implementation of your intentional actions. As a couple, you must make a new commitment of dedication, effort, and a willingness to adapt and grow together as partners. Make sure that you can stand firm when challenges arise and not allow them to knock you off your center.

Furthermore, it is through the transformative process that your relationship will evolve from mere aspirations to living and fulfilling experiences. You will witness the impact of your individual and collective intentional efforts as they advance emotional intimacy, reduce challenges, and give you more to celebrate through your shared accomplishments. The alignment of inspired intentions with purposeful steps creates a positive relational feedback loop, reinforcing the bond and resilience of the relationship over time.

∞∞∞

Implementing inspired action in your relationship requires that you be conscious and deliberate in your expressions of love, appreciation, and empathy. A proactive approach is needed. Through your conscious choices, you support your relationship through kind gestures, words, and thoughtful acts that promote affection and appreciation. This does not require any actions to be implemented by your partner before you become a willing participant. Quite the contrary, you must take the necessary actionable steps to align yourself with your inspirational desires for your relationship, then follow intuition into manifesting those desires.

Practical Insight: You must first decide, because it is a choice, to let go of all past seemingly inadequacies, hurtful actions, disappointments, hurt, and resentment. Your mindset is the change agent. If you are occupied with the old ways of thinking and feeling, then creating new habits, ideas, and goals for your relationship will never take root. You must fully and completely release whatever is keeping you from achieving your full relationship potential. What we constantly think about, we constantly get. Wanting your partner to change before any of these things are established is basing your change on false pretenses.

MANIFEST A JOY-FILLED RELATIONSHIP

Nothing outside of you needs to change first. Everything required to manifest a joy-filled relationship is found within.

Practices/Techniques/Exercises

- ❖ Inspired action often begins with improved communication. You can practice active listening, express appreciation and gratitude, share vulnerabilities, and engage in open and honest dialogue about your desires, goals, and concerns.

- ❖ What it doesn't mean: Constantly interrupting, finger-pointing, placing blame, arguing your point, holding back true feelings, and being dishonest.

- ❖ Purposeful steps include creating opportunities for shared experiences that align with inspired intentions. This may involve planning romantic outings, engaging in shared hobbies or interests (of one partner or both, be open to switching it up), or trying something new to create adventure and take you out of the same old ways of doing things. Be inspired to ask friends for ideas, look up the latest trends that are age-appropriate, do things that you enjoyed from the past, or recreate a fond memory of shared love and romance to forge new bonds and create lasting memories.

- ❖ What it doesn't mean: Always expecting your partner to engage in activities you enjoy. Continuously doing what you have always done. Refusing to try something because you believe you won't like it. Not being open to new adventures. Unwilling to change.

- ❖ Small gestures of kindness, thoughtfulness, and support can significantly impact restoring love one act at a time. These can range from simple acts like preparing a favorite meal, picking up your partner's favorite snack while at the store, offering a listening ear during challenging times, surprising each other with meaningful gifts or gestures of affection, or staying home and being intentionally present in a shared activity.

- ❖ What it doesn't mean: Acts of service and thoughtfulness do not imply that you should compromise your own needs or well-being for the sake of your partner. It also doesn't mean performing these acts with the expectation of immediate reciprocation or using them to manipulate or control your partner. The essence of these gestures lies in their genuine and selfless nature, aimed at nurturing the relationship rather than keeping score or seeking validation. Balance is key; both partners should engage in these thoughtful acts to foster mutual respect and affection, ensuring that the relationship remains healthy and supportive for both individuals.

- ❖ Inspired action also encompasses empathy and understanding. Partners can actively seek to understand each other's perspectives, validate emotions, and offer support and encouragement during both joyful moments and difficult times.

- ❖ What it doesn't mean: Ignoring or dismissing your partner's feelings, invalidating their experiences, pretending to listen while thinking about your response, showing impatience, or refusing to see things from their perspective. Empathy and understanding require genuine effort, openness, and a commitment to connect on a deeper emotional level, in short, emotional intelligence.

By incorporating these practices into your daily interactions, you will develop a culture of inspiration, appreciation, and growth. With conscious and deliberate implementation, inspired action becomes a natural and enriching part of your shared journey.

∞∞∞

Sustaining a fulfilling connection in your relationship requires ongoing dedication and effort. Purposeful steps based on inspiration are not a one-time endeavor but a continuous commitment. This involves you intentionally and deliberately building upon the basis of inspired actions and intentional steps so that you can create a consistent and nurturing environment. Here are some key elements you can use to sustain your connection.

- ❖ Commit to sustaining a fulfilling connection and recognize that relationships evolve and require continuous growth. They are open to learning from experiences, addressing challenges collaboratively, and adapting their approaches to meet changing needs and aspirations. This adaptability and open-mindedness are key to maintaining a healthy and vibrant relationship.

❖ Establishing regular check-ins or communication practices allows partners to stay connected and attuned to each other's thoughts, feelings, and goals. These check-ins provide opportunities to celebrate successes, address concerns, and recalibrate priorities as needed.

❖ Inspired actions contribute to building emotional intimacy, which is essential for a fulfilling connection. This involves sharing vulnerabilities, expressing affection, creating a safe space for authentic expression, and being honest, which means telling the truth without judgment, fear, or later repercussions. Being able to hear and handle difficult situations through emotional intelligence and growth.

❖ Sustaining a fulfilling connection requires striking a balance between individual autonomy and shared experiences. Partners respect each other's independence while actively participating in joint activities, decision-making processes, and life goals that align with their collective vision. The joy of shared experiences, from simple moments to grand adventures, is a testament to the strength of your bond. The growth of one partner contributes to the growth of the partnership. Realizing that support for each other supports the relationship as a whole.

If you consistently integrate these elements into your relationship development, you will reinforce the foundation of trust, mutual respect, and emotional connection. Whereby sustaining a fulfilling connection becomes a collaborative and rewarding journey of growth and shared experiences.

∞∞∞

When you become entirely open to purposeful steps rooted in inspiration, you will have laid the groundwork for lasting love and happiness. You will have formed a resilient relationship that can withstand and continue to flourish amidst challenges.

Creating a safe and supportive environment where both partners can be vulnerable promotes emotional intimacy and strengthens your bond. It involves openness, empathy, and a devotion to sharing fears, hopes, and dreams without reserve. Despite previous or societal beliefs around vulnerability, you are willing to open up and share your true feelings without defending or opposing issues. This may be a new space for you or your partner. Be patient and give yourself or your partner time to unfold naturally.

Trust is the building block of relationship longevity. Partners build trust through consistent positive actions, honesty, reliability, and transparency. Trust allows individuals to feel secure, valued, and understood within the relationship regardless of the past. With both partners' total and unwavering commitment to rebuilding broken trust through forgiveness, heart-felt apologies, accountability, honesty, reliability, and transparency, relationships can thrive again. Both partners must be willing to release and forgive past mistakes forever. This allows partners to be guided by love and hope instead of pain and fear. Rebuilding requires a willingness to be vulnerable and plant new seeds of relational possibilities.

Strong relationships endure challenges with resilience and mutual support. Partners navigate obstacles, disagreements, and life transitions with empathy, communication, and a shared commitment to overcoming difficulties together. You achieve this by viewing you and your partner as a united front against challenges rather than as individuals on opposite sides defending your positions.

Resilience, the ability to approach problems as a team, focus on the issue at hand, and devise the best plan of action for the relationship, is crucial. It stems from the understanding that there are no winners and losers in intimate relationships; what affects one partner affects both. If one loses, the entire relationship loses.

Building a strong foundation for lasting love involves a mindset of lifelong learning and growth. Partners must embrace opportunities for personal and relational development – such as this book, seek positive feedback, and evolve together. Relationship stagnation can result from routine and monotony, communication breakdown, neglecting intimacy, personal growth disparity, lack of shared goals, unaddressed issues, external stressors, a loss of fun and playfulness, unrealistic expectations, or recent dependency on technology. Personal and relational development brings a heightened awareness to address issues differently for positive results and change. You cannot solve a problem at the conscious level in which it was created; you do not have the capacity, knowledge, or wisdom. If you did, you would not have experienced the challenge.

When embodying these principles and actively investing in your relationship, you'll enjoy the benefits of lasting love, mutual satisfaction, and a common sense of purpose. Building a solid foundation for happiness and enduring connection demands commitment, patience, and a profound appreciation for the shared path of marriage or partnership.

∞∞∞

Periods of inertia (sluggishness) can be all too familiar in long-term relationships, especially in marriage. Those moments where progress seems stalled and you feel stuck in stagnation are periods when understanding the changing aspects of relationship growth is important. Overcoming inertia demands awareness, courage, flexibility, and dedication to evolving together, no matter what. As we like to say, "You have to be in it to win it!"

Although relationships may encounter some of the same issues, no two relationships are the same. While inspiration sparks the vision for change, fundamental transformation happens when you can push past inertia and take positive steps in establishing your desires.

Shared story

Earl and Angela's journey is a testament to the transformative power of inspired action within relationships. Initially, their marriage faced challenges typical of many long-term partnerships: unspoken resentments, unmet expectations, and a sense of disconnection. Recognizing the need for change from a deep inner longing for more, they set out to get answers to their relationship challenges. This included the importance of self-discovery, couples coaching, and engaging in heartfelt conversations. Inspired by a shared intuitive vision of a happy future, they took deliberate steps towards healing, apologizing for past hurts, and rekindling their passion through acts of kindness and affection. This recognition was the first inspired action they took - a conscious decision to confront their issues rather than let them fester. Over time, their relationship blossomed again, strengthened by a newfound sense of love and passion.

Their journey began with a commitment to self-discovery. They sought guidance through couples coaching, where they learned valuable communication skills and gained insights into each other's perspectives. This allowed them to set shared and personal goals that aligned with their values. This phase of their journey highlights the importance of seeking external support and being open to learning and mutual growth as individuals and as a couple.

Inspired by a shared intuitive vision of a happy future filled with love and passion, Earl and Angela took deliberate steps toward healing from the inside out. They engaged in heartfelt conversations, where they expressed their thoughts, feelings, and vulnerabilities honestly. This open and authentic communication laid the foundation for rebuilding trust and insight in their relationship. They took turns planning weekly meaningful and connecting activities that opened them up to new perspectives and enjoyment.

Apologizing for past hurts was a critical moment in their journey. It required humility, empathy, and a willingness to take responsibility for their actions. This act of apology wasn't just about words but was followed by tangible changes in behavior - shared and individual meditation practices, acts of kindness, and affection that demonstrated their commitment to rebuilding their marriage and strengthening their newly formed bond.

Over time, they developed a deeper sense of compassion and acceptance for each other's needs and desires. This newfound connection was not built overnight but through consistent efforts, awareness, and a shared commitment to mutual growth and happiness.

Earl and Angela's story is just one example of how applying proven relationship techniques, tailored strategies, and inner intuition can lead to positive transformations in relationships.

Many of the stories we share encompass diverse scenarios, from couples rediscovering passion after years of monotony to individuals navigating complex relationship challenges with grace and resilience. By sharing these stories, we aim to showcase the universal nature of inspired action - which is not limited by age, background, or relationship stage. Instead, it is a principle that anyone can apply to create meaningful change in their relationship.

We also introduce behavioral and positive psychology strategies, offering insights into common hurdles that hinder progress in relationships. We go further by providing techniques and emphasizing the importance of implementing micro-actions to empower you to break through inertia and kickstart positive transformations. You can overcome anything if you 1) make the decision to and 2) take the necessary actions to achieve your desired transformation. No one can make the decision or do the work for you. Although this journey is traveled together as partners, it requires you to put in your own work for your own results. Therefore, if you are constantly thinking about your partner and insisting that they read this book, then you really have some personal work to do. You need to stop deflecting, look in the mirror, and say, "This is for me. I need awareness and change first - so get started, self; you have work to do."

∞∞∞

One of the significant ways this law manifests in relationships is through communication. Unresolved issues, inability to effectively resolve the same conflicts, and unhealthy communication styles can sway your decision to give up. Seeing no way out or no change can cause you to stop caring and turn away, making this an unbearable obstacle to face. Especially if you believe you have tried over and over again to communicate this to your partner.

To overcome this hurdle and prevent communication barriers from destroying your relationship, you must learn the skill of communication. Communication is a skill that, if not developed, can cause issues in all your relationships, not just your romantic ones.

Usually, effectively communicating needs to be correctly understood and taught. We may passively pick up what we think is right or wrong but lack accurate, practical communication skills. Understanding that communication is a skill is the first process in overcoming obstacles. Effective communication is the basis for building understanding, trust, and emotional intelligence.

When you learn to actively engage in open and honest communication, sharing your needs, desires, and concerns, you acquire the necessary skills to deepen your connections and strengthen bonds without fearing retaliation, blame, or misunderstandings. By developing your communication skills to take intentional steps, such as active listening, validating each other's feelings, and communicating clearly, you will be able to successfully infuse conflict resolution that will nurture a sense of security and mutual support within your relationship.

However, when you don't communicate and allow challenges such as fear, self-doubt, and complacency to influence your thinking and emotions, they impede your progress and prevent you from taking inspired action.

Fear of vulnerability may prevent you or your partner from expressing your true feelings and desires stemming from past rejection or previous dismissal of feelings. When you constantly tell yourself why your fears are valid, fear can be a significant barrier to taking meaningful action. Our natural instinct is to protect ourselves from potential harm or rejection.

However, in your relationship, fear can show up as an unwillingness to express vulnerabilities, share genuine feelings, or address sensitive issues. Overcoming obstacles requires a shift in mindset, which views vulnerability as a strength rather than a weakness. You can improve trust and intimacy by creating a judgment-free zone for open dialogue, no matter the topic or level of sensitivity, where each one feels accepted and supported regardless of their vulnerabilities.

Being able to be vulnerable is where listening and speaking as a skill become a top priority. You must be able to actively listen to what your partner is saying, not what you think they are saying or listening to respond. Speaking in a manner of self-awareness and change instead of blame and resentment.

THE LAW OF INSPIRED ACTION

You must be able to confront old issues in new, mature ways. That's why recognizing and practicing specific techniques in those significantly weak areas in your relationship is essential.

There comes a time in every relationship when troubles are a present and clear danger. During those times, self-doubt can rear its ugly head and manufacture thoughts of uncertainty over the relationship's future. Self-doubt will cast doubts on your abilities, decisions, and the relationship's viability. If not careful, it can lead to second-guessing your actions, hesitating in making commitments or questioning your worthiness of love and happiness.

Overcoming self-doubt involves building self-confidence through self-awareness, self-compassion, and positive self-talk. Taking the necessary time to love yourself can prove to be invaluable in overcoming obstacles that you thought were impossible for you to overcome. Strengthening your self-confidence and self-love opens you up to being able to receive and support each other in challenging self-limiting beliefs, providing reassurance, and celebrating each other's strengths and accomplishments more often. Visit our website for a free downloadable PDF or audio version of denials and affirmations.

Complacency stems from familiarity, which may lead to indifference and a loss of passion. Complacency often arises from a sense of comfort or routine in the relationship. While familiarity can be reassuring, it can also lead to stagnation and a lack of growth or excitement. Overcoming complacency requires conscious efforts to inject newness, spontaneity, and happy shared experiences into the relationship. This may involve trying new activities together, setting mutual goals, or revisiting old passions to reignite the spark. Regular communication about evolving needs and desires can help prevent complacency from settling in.

Inspired action also encompasses an awareness of timing. This law encourages you to synchronize your efforts with the natural rhythms of life, recognizing when to initiate movement and when to pause for reflection or growth. Imagine a surfer waiting for the perfect wave - his timing is crucial for seizing the most opportune moment.

Similarly, in your relationship, inspired action involves trusting that opportunities unfold when the time is right, not forced. Often, when couples are experiencing issues, they have a list of things they want their partner to change. However, in this book, we will continually and emphatically stress that your partner will change when they become aware of what they need to change. You do your part on your time and allow your partner to shift, move, and change according to their understanding and desires for the relationship. Working from within will allow the process to manifest in the outer. You don't need to tell your partner where they need to change or vice versa. Once you have done the work on yourself, you will be better equipped to have open, effective, and honest communication from a higher level of consciousness, opening up opportunities to see and offer new approaches to old issues.

Consider an analogy of a rolling snowball gathering size and speed as it moves downhill. Inspired action creates momentum, propelling you towards your relationship goals. Moreover, when you tune in to honoring your inner truths and communicating openly with your partner, the value of your relationship will escalate to new enjoyable heights. You will be an active part in creating a space where both you and your partner feel comfortable expressing yourselves authentically without fear of judgment or rejection because you have witnessed the snowball effect in what you have built together.

∞∞∞

Inspired action is closely linked to having a clear vision and actionable goals within your relationship. You can benefit from setting shared goals that align with your values, aspirations, and vision for the future. Breaking down these goals into manageable steps makes them more achievable and establishes a sense of progress and accomplishment. Regularly revisiting and revising goals allows adaptability and ensures that both partners remain invested in their shared journey.

Mindfulness practices can significantly enhance your ability to take inspired action in your relationships. By cultivating present-moment awareness, you can better understand your thoughts, emotions, and reactions. Mindfulness also promotes empathy, compassion, and nonjudgmental acceptance.

Sometimes, overcoming obstacles may require external support or guidance. Traditionally, couples counseling or therapy were couples-only options, which have their time and place. Nevertheless, with couples seeking more out of their relationships and happiness longevity, other practices came about. Relationship Coaching has given couples a higher awareness of what it takes to create and sustain thriving relationships. Coaching is necessary in helping couples acquire the education and skills they need to play and win the relationship game.

Too often, it's not the marriage but the individual skills couples lack in communication, conflict resolution, empathy, and emotional maturity (intelligence). Realizing that couples lack the skills they need to be successful in marriage, relationship coaches offer more in-depth training, skill building, action-taking, and couple-specific approaches to everyday issues. Through relational coaching, couples learn how to create a safe space to effectively work through challenges, improve communication skills, learn effective problem-solving strategies, forgive and release blame, reignite passion, and overcome issues through empathy. Inspired action acts as a vehicle to overcome obstacles, setting the wheels of positive change in motion.

Other viable support can come from trusted friends with a proven track record, mentors, marriage clubs, marriage groups, or support groups that can also offer valuable insights and encouragement. Visit our website at legendaryrelationship.com for couples coaching and personal development; book a discovery call today to see how we can help you create a thriving and lasting love affair with yourself and your partner.

∞∞∞∞

To transcend inertia, you must first acknowledge its presence and embrace the discomfort it brings. This acknowledgment opens you up to improving all areas of your relationship, encouraging an environment where fears and doubts can be shared without judgment. Such openness lays the groundwork for taking positive steps toward a happier future.

Below are strategies to assist you in overcoming inertia and initiating positive changes in your relationship. These strategies include practical exercises, mindfulness techniques, and self-reflection practices to break through inertia.

THE LAW OF INSPIRED ACTION

- ❖ Begin by identifying specific goals or areas of improvement within your relationship. These could include improving communication, developing or rebuilding trust, enhancing intimacy, or working towards common aspirations such as travel or career milestones.

- ❖ Once goals are identified, break them down into smaller, manageable steps. For example, if the goal is to improve communication, actionable steps could include setting aside dedicated time for meaningful conversations, practicing active listening techniques, and expressing thoughts and feelings openly.

- ❖ Assign a timeline or deadline for each step to ensure urgency and accountability. This will help you stay focused and committed to your progress.

- ❖ Determine what resources are needed to achieve each step. This could involve scheduling coaching sessions, enrolling in a relationship course, or attending communication and emotional intelligence workshops. Visit our website at legendaryrelationship.com for upcoming seminars, workshops, books, our premium course, and other resources.

- ❖ Review progress on the action plan regularly and be willing to adjust strategies based on feedback and evolving needs. Flexibility and adaptability are key to navigating challenges and staying on course to achieve the desired outcomes.

- Alongside breaking goals into actionable steps, define clear milestones that signify progress towards the overarching goal. These milestones should be specific, measurable, and attainable within a reasonable timeframe.

- Celebrate reaching each milestone as it indicates progress and success in your journey. Celebrations can be simple yet meaningful, such as a special date night, writing appreciation notes to each other, or engaging in activities that bring joy and laughter.

- Use milestone moments as opportunities for reflection and learning. Discuss what worked well, what challenges were faced, and how strategies can be refined moving forward. Learning from each milestone helps improve the action plan and stay motivated.

- Sometimes, reaching a milestone may reveal new insights or shifts in priorities. Be open to adjusting goals or setting new milestones based on the evolving dynamics of the relationship and individual growth.

- Develop an attitude of openness to feedback from your partner and the outcomes of your actions. Feedback provides valuable insight into what works and what may need adjustments in your approach.

- ❖ Be willing to adapt your strategies and plans based on feedback and changing circumstances. Flexibility allows you to pivot when needed rather than rigidly sticking to a course that may not yield the desired results.

- ❖ Stay open to exploring new opportunities that may arise along the way. These opportunities could be new ways to connect with your partner, personal growth possibilities, or resources supporting your goals.

- ❖ Practice mindfulness in decision-making by pausing to reflect on the potential consequences of your actions. Consider how your decisions align with your values, goals, and relationship well-being.

- ❖ Develop self-awareness to better recognize and trust your intuition. This involves tuning into your feelings, thoughts, and bodily sensations to gain insights into what feels right or aligned with your deeper intentions.

- ❖ Learn to differentiate between intuition and fear-based impulses. Intuition often comes from a place of inner wisdom and alignment with your values. At the same time, fear-driven decisions may stem from past experiences or limiting beliefs.

- ❖ Actively listen to your inner guidance without judgment or immediate dismissal. Sometimes, intuitive insights may not seem logical at first but can lead to significant breakthroughs when acted upon with trust.

- ❖ Test your intuitive insights by taking small steps and observing the outcomes. This testing and validation process builds confidence in your intuition over time, making it a reliable guide in making inspired choices.

- ❖ A growth mindset involves viewing challenges as opportunities for learning and growth rather than obstacles. Encourage each other to see difficulties as stepping stones toward personal and relational development.

- ❖ Instead of viewing setbacks as failures, reframe them as valuable lessons. Discuss what can be learned from setbacks and how they can inform future actions and decisions.

- ❖ Emphasize the importance of effort and persistence in achieving goals. Recognize and celebrate the effort put into taking inspired actions, regardless of immediate outcomes.

- ❖ Implement a culture of continuous learning and skill development within the relationship. This can involve attending workshops or courses together, reading books on personal growth and relationship dynamics, or seeking guidance from mentors or coaches.

- ❖ Express self-compassion by being kind and understanding toward oneself during challenges and setbacks. Recognize that personal growth is a journey with ups and downs, and self-compassion plays a crucial role in maintaining motivation and resilience. Moreover, note that regret and self-condemnation are cripplers to further growth and elevation.

- ❖ Encourage healthy risk-taking within the relationship, where partners feel supported in trying new things and stepping outside their comfort zones. Taking calculated risks can lead to new experiences, insights, and opportunities to rekindle excitement.

- ❖ Regularly reflect on personal and relational growth experiences. Discuss how individual growth contributes to the overall well-being and vitality of the relationship, reinforcing the importance of a growth mindset in creating a thriving partnership.

Incorporating these detailed strategies of embracing flexibility and trusting your intuition, you can decrease challenges, seize growth opportunities, and reestablish deeper intimate connections based on mutuality and authenticity.

Celebrate not only the end results but also the progress made along the way. Acknowledge and appreciate the small steps taken toward positive change as they contribute to the overall growth and strengthening of your relationship.

Through successful implementation you can create an action plan and set milestones to more effectively enjoy your journey, stay motivated, and track your progress. Developing a growth mindset can encourage flexibility, adaptability, and a shared commitment to continuous elevation. This mindset supports inspired action and establishes a positive and empowering framework for building a thriving and fulfilling relationship.

"An idea not coupled with action will never get any bigger than the brain cell it occupied." - Arnold H. Glasow

Glasow's insight encapsulates the essence of the Law of Inspired Action. It challenges us to bridge the gap between inspiration and reality through purposeful and consistent effort. By embracing this principle, you can propel your relationship forward, transcending mere ideas and entering the realm of tangible transformation.

Furthermore, the Law of Inspired Action encourages you to take proactive steps to address challenges and conflicts in your relationship. Rather than avoiding or suppressing issues, you can engage in constructive dialogue, seek mutual understanding, and work together to find solutions. By approaching disagreements with empathy, compassion, and a dedication to cooperation, you can effectively strive towards strengthening your partnership and deepening your emotional connection forever.

In *Golden Spiritual Nuggets* by Rev. Shirley Lawson (2009) she reminds us, "Live to be consciously aware of your every thought, for thoughts eventually become things."

Chapter Four
THE LAW OF CORRESPONDENCE
The Mirroring Nature in Relationships

Welcome aboard your expedition through the corridors of relational dynamics, where the Law of Correspondence serves as both a directional light and a transformative force. In this chapter's expansive exploration, you will uncover the elaborate interplay between the various layers of existence, revealing the echoes that shape your self-discovery and relational evolution. Have you packed your open-mindedness for this leg of the flight, where you will explore and understand the universal law that governs human connections? As we prepare for takeoff, remember you are here to learn how to soar to new heights in your relationship. So, if you're ready, let's ascend together to greater altitudes of awareness.

As you learn about the Law of Correspondence, you will begin to recognize universal oneness and truth in the phrase "As above, so below; as below, so above." In the big picture of life, the Law of Correspondence shows how the vast universe and the tiny details of our lives are interconnected. "What's up there is reflected down here, and what's down here is reflected up there." - this old idea invites you to see how everything in the universe is linked, from the stars to your daily experiences.

MANIFEST A JOY-FILLED RELATIONSHIP

This chapter reveals the mirroring nature of the Law of Correspondence within the context of your relationship. Revealing how the dynamics and energies at play on one level of your relationship reflect and influence those on another. The Law of Correspondence is a principle in metaphysics and spirituality, suggesting a correspondence between different levels of existence. When applied to your relationship, it encourages couples to recognize the interconnectedness between their individual actions and the harmony or disharmony within their relationship. By understanding and aligning with this law, you can gain clarity on your relational dynamics and take steps toward improving your connection, harmony, and consistency.

When you seek to understand and intentionally shape the resonances between the different levels of your existence, you can become open and receptive to the power of correspondence through self-discovery and relational transformation. You can discover the Law of Correspondence for yourself, as it gives you a deeper look into the universal law governing human dynamics, uncovering the parallels between your inner world of mind action and your outer manifestations. That means the connection between what you think and what is happening in your life. All things are manifestations, so if there is something in your life or relationship that you are not happy with, you must recognize there was a thought that created it and brought it forth from the invisible to your visible experience.

∞∞∞

At its foundation, the Law of Correspondence suggests there is a direct correlation between the patterns and dynamics present in your inner world and those observed in your external interactions and experiences. By understanding this principle,

THE LAW OF CORRESPONDENCE

you can gain awareness of the underlying dynamics within your relationship, helping you move beyond surface-level conflicts and challenges to address the root causes and initiate lasting change.

The Law of Correspondence holds reflective implications for your relationship. The dynamics you encounter in your connections with your partner often serve as mirrors reflecting the patterns within yourself. Consider a scenario where conflicts arise in your relationship. Rather than attributing blame externally, the Law of Correspondence encourages you to examine the internal patterns and beliefs contributing to external challenges. By addressing and transforming these inner correspondences, you pave the way for synchronization and growth in your relationship.

This motivates you to examine your own thought patterns, emotional responses, and belief systems and recognize how these internal factors shape your perceptions and interactions with your partner. By engaging in self-awareness and introspection, you begin to realize the subtle ways in which your internal world mirrors and directly influences your dynamics. Awareness is crucial in manifesting.

As you explore the depths of this law, you will discover the emphasis put on the importance of assuming personal responsibility for one's inner self, challenging you to recognize instances where blame is placed on external factors or your partner. Instead, you are urged to take ownership of your thoughts, emotions, and behaviors, acknowledging your role in creating your personal experiences.

Through your examination, you are empowered to become aware of self-discovery and expansion and look at the trenches of your own psyche and the intricacies of your relationship. Once you acknowledge this concept, you can start to understand and implement the Law of Correspondence into your relationship. By addressing and being open to changing your internal correspondences, you can intentionally create opportunities for alignment and growth to get the relationship you want and desire.

∞∞∞

We looked at psychological research and systemic thinking to fully understand the connection between individual experiences and broader relational dynamics. For example, the family systems theory (FST) is a psychological and therapeutic approach that views the family as an interconnected, dynamic system where each member's behavior affects and is affected by the behavior of others. Developed by Murray Bowen, this theory emphasizes the importance of understanding the family as a whole rather than focusing on individual members in isolation. It suggests that family interaction patterns can influence each member's emotional and psychological well-being and that issues are best addressed by examining and improving the relational dynamics. For instance, studies on FST help shed light on how the patterns established in your family of origin can show up in your adult relationships, thereby illustrating the correspondence between the different stages in your life.

This multidisciplinary approach allows you to start to bridge the gap between your individual experiences and broader actions, influences, and behaviors that shape your relationship. You are invited to expand your knowledge as you explore the value of psychological research and systemic thinking

THE LAW OF CORRESPONDENCE

regarding your relationship levels. This will enable you to understand how patterns originating from your family can move through and influence your adult relationships. It serves as a reminder of the deep-seated connection between different stages of your life and the patterns that thread you together, repeating across generations and your relational context.

When you venture into this awareness, you will often find yourself in the subtle pull of give-and-take, understanding that balance must be at the heart of sustainable love and deep connection. This will guide you as you direct the ups and downs of energy within your relationship, discerning the delicate balance between your individual needs and the collective well-being of the partnership. As you learn to accept the wisdom of this law, you will unlock its secrets and become better at harmonizing your energies and creating an environment where love, joy, and growth can flourish organically regardless of familial patterns and past experiences.

∞∞∞∞

The law of correspondence invites you to examine how your personal beliefs, unbalanced emotions, negative habits, and erroneous thinking patterns are reflected in the shared space of your relationship. Can you entertain the idea that the dynamics within your relationship often resemble what is going on internally?

By examining your personal beliefs, emotional responses, and thought patterns, you will see how they play out in your relationship. The law serves as a mirror, revealing the interaction between your personal and shared relational dynamics. You are encouraged to explore recurring themes or challenges within your relationship. By recognizing patterns, you realize the energetic reflections at play, shedding light on the underlying forces at work that shape or have shaped your connection.

As you connect your personal experiences with universal frequency, you'll find yourself deeply reflecting on inner and outer realities. You will discover how every thought, emotion, and action you engage in contributes to the tightly constructed experiences that reflect the energetic patterns of the universe. Just as planets move in precise orbits, your life unfolds in resonance with the energetic frequencies you emit.

Imagine a tranquil pond perfectly reflecting the beauty of its surroundings. If the surface of the water is calm, the reflection is clear and undistorted. Similarly, when you improve your inner harmony and align with positive vibrations, your external reality mirrors harmony and fulfillment. Consequently, if you embody inner chaos and attune yourself to negative vibrations, your external reality mirrors a life of disharmony and discord, "As within, so without; as without, so within."

Applying the Law of Correspondence in your relationship requires a keen awareness of patterns and reflections. Recognizing the patterns in your thought process enlightens you about the underlying behaviors that shape your interactions with your partner. Identifying relational patterns is essential for developing a thriving connection. When you apply the law to this aspect of your life, you begin to recognize that the undercurrents within your relationship mirror the patterns and energies in the universe. This self-awareness becomes an essential tool for intentional change, enabling alignment of the inner world with the higher vibrational frequencies of the universe.

THE LAW OF CORRESPONDENCE

We can safely say that everyone encounters challenges in their relationship. When you use the law, you intentionally and actively begin to note patterns of disharmony within your interactions. This allows you to start looking at that disharmony from your emotional state, seeking to understand and transform those inner patterns that are reflected in your external experiences. This process becomes a form of personal alchemy, turning discord into accord. The good news is that you don't have to struggle with trial and error, there are tools that can help you- if you use them.

Therapeutic techniques, such as narrative therapy, systemic constellation, self-reflection, and journaling can be valuable tools for identifying and understanding patterns in your relationship.

Narrative therapy, for example, invites you to explore the stories you tell yourself about your relationship and how these narratives shape your interactions. Examining these stories can uncover underlying beliefs and assumptions influencing your behaviors.

Through the systemic constellation approach, you can map out the dynamics of your relationship system, including the roles each partner plays. By visualizing these patterns, you understand the systemic forces influencing your relationship and identify areas for growth and change.

Self-reflection and journaling are instrumental tools for introspection, where you can gain clarity on your personal thoughts, emotions, and behaviors, allowing you to easily identify recurring patterns and themes. Journaling can also serve as an indispensable tool for tracking progress and observing shifts in relational dynamics over time.

In addition to therapeutic techniques, you can benefit from seeking constructive feedback from trusted friends, family members, therapists, or relationship coaches who can offer an outside perspective on your relationship dynamics. These individuals can provide respected insights and observations that may not be apparent to you, helping you recognize and understand your relational patterns. However, the key is not in asking or seeking feedback but in being open to receiving it.

Therefore, awareness becomes the initial step toward transformation and manifestation. This is followed by equipping yourself with the necessary tools to recognize recurring patterns in your relationship for self-growth and lasting positive change. These techniques offer valuable insights into the intergenerational patterns that may be influencing your current connection. Through awareness, you begin to make transformative shifts in your relational dynamics by adequately using one or all of these techniques.

Practices/Techniques/Exercises for Awareness

Narrative therapy techniques are therapeutic approaches that help you reshape your personal narratives and adopt a more positive and empowering self-identity. It also focuses on the stories you tell yourself about your family and life. Michael White and David Epston developed this technique in an approach to help people identify and rewrite negative or unhelpful narratives and create more positive life stories. It emphasizes the role of stories in shaping identity and experiences.

This therapy views you as separate from your problems and encourages you to rewrite your story not as you may have first viewed it but in ways that highlight your strengths and abilities.

For example, it invites partners to explore the stories they tell themselves about their relationship and how these narratives shape their interactions. By examining these stories, you can uncover deep-rooted beliefs and assumptions that negatively influence your thinking, behavior, and reactions.

Key Techniques in Narrative Therapy

1. Externalization, which involves separating you from your problem(s). Instead of seeing the problem(s) as an inherent part of you, therapists or coaches can help you see it as an external issue that can be addressed. For example, instead of saying "I am depressed," a person might be encouraged to say, "Depression is affecting me." This helps reduce self-blame and opens you up to new possibilities for change.

2. Deconstruction, which involves breaking down and examining dominant stories to understand how they shape your perception of yourself and your world. This helps you unpack these narratives to reveal hidden assumptions and influences. For example, a person might explore how cultural expectations about gender roles have shaped their identity and choices, and then create a more individualized and authentic self-narrative.

3. Re-authoring, which encourages you to create new, more empowering narratives about your life. This

might involve identifying your strengths, achievements, and positive experiences that have been overshadowed by dominant problem-saturated stories. For instance, a person might reframe their narrative from "I am not very smart and always do stupid things." to "I have overcome many challenges and learned valuable lessons that can positively contribute to the value of my relationship and life."

4. Unique Outcomes, which involves identifying and focusing on moments in your life when the problem did not dominate or when you responded to the problem in a way that showed resilience and strength. For example, recall a time when you felt confident and successful despite ongoing anxiety. Where you can look back and see that you were pulling from inner strength instead of outer experiences.

Examples

- ❖ A person might have struggled with anger and worked to see anger as a "bully" that they can stand up to and manage, rather than seeing themselves as inherently angry.

- ❖ As an adult dealing with feelings of inadequacy, you might explore and challenge the societal expectations and family beliefs that contribute to your feelings, recognizing them as external pressures rather than personal failures.

- ❖ Someone might view themselves as "a victim of circumstances" and might be guided to reframe their narrative to "a survivor who has navigated and overcome significant obstacles."

- ❖ A person with low self-esteem might be encouraged to focus on a specific instance when they felt proud of their accomplishments, such as completing a challenging project.

Narrative therapy thus empowers you to take control of your stories and, consequently, your life.

Systemic constellation work, also known as family constellation work, is a therapeutic approach developed by Bert Hellinger. It involves you exploring and resolving unconscious patterns and dynamics within your family system or relational system. Through this approach, you can map out the dynamics of your relationship system, including the roles each partner plays and the underlying dynamics at play. By visualizing these patterns, you gain insight into the systemic forces influencing your relationship and identify areas for growth and change. The goal is to bring hidden influences to light and promote healing and resolution of issues that may be affecting your well-being, consciously or unconsciously.

1. Setting up the constellation involves creating a physical representation of the issue, family system, or relational system. Participants (often group members or objects) are chosen to represent family members or relational elements of the issue and are positioned in relation to one another in the space.

2. Representative Perception is where representatives often experience feelings and insights that reflect the emotions and dynamics of the actual people they are representing. This phenomenon helps reveal hidden truths and unresolved tensions within the system or issue.

3. The coach or therapist guides the representatives through movements, statements, or re-positioning to bring about a sense of balance, resolution, and harmony within the system. This can involve acknowledging past traumas, expressing unspoken feelings, or restoring broken connections.

4. Healing Statements are suggested where participants are encouraged to voice specific statements that can facilitate healing and reconciliation, such as expressions of forgiveness, acknowledgment of suffering, or declarations of love and respect.

Examples

❖ An individual struggling with chronic anxiety might set up a constellation representing their family. Representatives for family members might reveal underlying patterns of unexpressed grief or loyalty to a deceased relative. Through guided movements and statements, these hidden dynamics are addressed, helping the individual find peace and relief from anxiety.

- Someone facing difficulty in romantic relationships might explore their family constellation to identify patterns from their family of origin influencing their current relationships. They might discover an unconscious loyalty to a parent's unfulfilled love life. Acknowledging and resolving these patterns can open the way for healthier relationships.

In systemic constellation work, a scenario where one partner feels anxiety and stress over choosing between taking the side of their parent or sibling over their spouse can be explored through a constellation setup. Here's how it might look:

Example - Participants

- Partner A: The person experiencing anxiety and stress (let's call them Jeremy).

- Partner B: Jeremy's spouse (let's call them Jamie).

- Parent: Jeremy's parent (let's call them Pat).

- Sibling: Jeremy's sibling (let's call them Sam).

Setting Up the Constellation

1. Jeremy explains his issue to us (relationship coaches): feeling torn between loyalty to Pat and Sam versus loyalty to Jamie, which causes anxiety and stress.

2. Representatives (or objects) are chosen to represent Jeremy, Jamie, Pat, and Sam. These representatives are then positioned in the space according to how Jeremy perceives their relationships. Typically, Jeremy might place himself in the center, with Pat and Sam on one side and Jamie on the other.

Representative Perception

❖ The representative for Jeremy might feel pulled in two directions, indicating the internal conflict.

❖ The representative for Jamie might feel isolated or unsupported, reflecting the strain in the marital relationship.

❖ The representatives for Pat and Sam might exhibit a strong, united front, which Jeremy feels obligated to align with, although Pat and Sam may not even be aware of the struggle.

Exploring Dynamics

➢ We then ask each representative to express their feelings and perceptions. For example:
➢ Jamie's representative might express feeling abandoned, not prioritized or supported.
➢ Pat's representative might express an expectation of loyalty from Jeremy.
➢ Sam's representative might feel a strong bond with Pat that excludes Jamie.

Resolution Movements

- ➤ We guide the representatives through movements or statements to address the tension. For instance:
- ➤ Jeremy's representative could face Pat and Sam and say, "I honor you as my family, but I need to stand with my spouse."
- ➤ Jamie's representative could move closer to Jeremy, symbolizing unity and support.

Healing Statements

- ➤ Representatives might be guided to voice specific statements that promote understanding.
- ➤ Jeremy to Pat and Sam: "I love you and respect our bond, but Jamie is my partner, and I need to prioritize our relationship."
- ➤ Pat to Jeremy: "We want you to be happy and support your relationship with Jamie."
- ➤ Jamie to Jeremy: "I understand your struggle and appreciate your efforts to balance these relationships and I don't want you to choose sides but love us all in a unique and respectful way that enhances family unity."

Through this process, the representatives and Jeremy might uncover hidden dynamics, such as unmet needs for approval or unspoken resentments. The guided movements and healing statements aim to create a more balanced and supportive relationship dynamic, reducing Jeremy's anxiety and stress.

In this constellation, Jeremy's internal conflict between familial loyalty and spousal commitment is externalized and explored. By addressing these relational dynamics, Jeremy can find a more harmonious way to navigate his relationships, reducing his anxiety and strengthening his bond with Jamie and his family.

Systemic constellation work aims to uncover and heal deep-seated relational dynamics, promoting greater love and emotional well-being in both personal and relational contexts.

Additionally, you can explore the concept of attachment styles as a framework for understanding relational patterns. Attachment theory suggests that your early experiences with caregivers shape your attachment styles and influence your patterns of relating in your adult relationship. By identifying your attachment style, you can uncover how your past experiences may be impacting your current relationship dynamics. This awareness can give way to greater empathy and understanding between you and your partner, allowing you to navigate challenges with compassion and grace.

The first tool for identifying patterns is self-reflection, a process that invites you and your partner to look deep into the recesses of your minds and hearts. Self-reflection serves as a starting point, offering you a mirror to examine your own thoughts, emotions, and behaviors within the context of your relationship - separately.

Practicing self-awareness or mindfulness is valuable for identifying and understanding relational patterns. Self-awareness and mindfulness involve bringing awareness to the present moment with an open and nonjudgmental attitude. You can practice self-awareness or mindfulness together through activities such as meditation, deep breathing exercises, or mindful communication. By developing self-awareness or mindfulness, you become more attuned to your thoughts, emotions, and relational dynamics, allowing you to respond to challenges with greater clarity and intentionality.

- ❖ **Meditation** - practice mindfulness or guided meditation sessions to center yourself and cultivate inner peace. Start with small increments of time and gradually increase.
  - ➢ **Benefit** - Meditation enhances self-awareness, reduces stress, and helps you approach your relationship with a calm and clear mind. It restores your natural energy and opens up the pathway for spiritual wholeness.

- ❖ **Self-Questioning** - regularly ask yourself reflective questions such as, "What do I truly want in my relationship?" or "How can I improve my communication with my partner?"
  - ➢ **Benefit** - This technique encourages deeper introspection and helps you understand your desires, needs, and areas for growth.

- ❖ **Visualization** - spend a few minutes each day visualizing your ideal relationship. Imagine positive interactions, mutual respect, and shared happiness. Visualize what it feels like and how your growth has contributed to the betterment of your relationship.

> **Benefit** - Visualization reinforces your goals and aspirations, helping you stay focused on manifesting a harmonious relationship. It lets the universe know what you want and brings it into the visible world.

- **Gratitude Practice** - reflect on and list the positive aspects of your relationship and express gratitude for them. This area is often overlooked. We are so busy focusing on what we want we forget to give thanks and be grateful for the pluses we already have.
  > **Benefit** - Practicing gratitude shifts your focus to the positive, fosters appreciation for your partner, and strengthens your relationship by nurturing a positive mindset. It also allows the universe to give you more to be grateful for.

Journaling involves writing down daily or weekly entries focusing on your thoughts, emotions, and experiences related to your relationship, paying close attention to the beliefs and behaviors surrounding those experiences. This practice allows you to reflect on your inner world and external interactions, helping you gain clarity and understanding of your relationship patterns. By putting your experiences into words, you create a tangible record that can reveal underlying patterns you might not notice at the moment. This awareness aids in transforming negative patterns into healthier, intentional ones for relationship growth and happiness.

THE LAW OF CORRESPONDENCE

- ❖ Dedicate a specific time each day or week to journal. Consistency is significant for gaining deeper insights.

- ❖ Find a quiet and comfortable place where you can write without interruptions. A safe space that allows you time to reflect and write down your revelations.

- ❖ Write freely without censoring yourself. Honesty is crucial for uncovering true patterns and feelings. Yet, make sure that your attention is on you and what part you play in the relationship patterns and reoccurring themes.

- ❖ Reflect on recent interactions with your partner. What emotions did you feel? What thoughts ran through your mind? How did you react? What could you have done differently?

- ❖ Over time, review your journal entries. Look for recurring themes, triggers, and behaviors that impact your relationship. What emotions or feelings were present and why? Were your feelings due in part to that incident or tied to past experiences that weren't resolved and discussed?

- ❖ Use prompts like, "What triggered this reaction?" or "How could I have responded differently?" to get a better understanding of YOU.

- Based on your insights, set small, achievable goals for changing negative patterns and enhancing positive interactions.

By journaling, you gain a clearer understanding of your relationship dynamics and empower yourself to make intentional, positive changes. This self-awareness advances growth, allowing you and your partner to build a stronger, deliberate foundation upon which to build by opening the door to mindful communication.

Practices/Techniques/Exercises for Communication

Mindful communication is key to accepting each other's perspectives and experiences. You engage in meaningful conversations about your relationship dynamics, exploring how your individual experiences are shaping your interactions. Active listening, empathy, and validation are essential components of effective mindful communication, allowing you the opportunity to truly connect and empathize with each other's experiences like never before.

- Active listening involves fully concentrating, understanding, and responding thoughtfully to what the other person is saying. You should focus entirely on your partner without interrupting, making them feel heard and valued.

- Maintain eye contact and nod occasionally to show you're engaged.

THE LAW OF CORRESPONDENCE

- ❖ Avoid interrupting or planning your response while your partner is speaking.

- ❖ Reflect back on what you heard by summarizing or paraphrasing their words. For example, you might say, "What I'm hearing is that you feel unprioritized when we don't spend time together."

- ❖ Avoid statements of blame or excuses. Stay focused on the topic at hand and communicate for comprehension and seeing from your partner's perspective. This doesn't mean you have to agree, active listening is for understanding and responding respectfully to what is being communicated.

Validating emotions means acknowledging and accepting your partner's feelings without judgment. This helps them feel understood and respected.

- ❖ Use phrases like "I understand what you're feeling." or "It makes sense that you're upset because."

- ❖ Avoid minimizing their feelings or jumping to problem-solving mode. Instead, show that you appreciate their perspective.

- ❖ For example, say, "I can see that you're feeling lonely because we haven't had much time together lately. That must be really hard for you."

Asking open-ended questions encourages your partner to share more about their thoughts and feelings, encouraging understanding and connection.

- ❖ Ask questions that cannot be answered with a simple "yes" or "no" This encourages your partner to elaborate and express themselves more fully.

- ❖ Examples include, "Can you tell me more about what's been bothering you?" or "How do you feel about our current situation?"

- ❖ Follow up with more questions based on their responses to show your genuine interest and support.

- ❖ Ask with genuine interest and support. Be aware and practice staying in control of your emotions.

By using these tools, you enhance empathetic listening in your relationship, opening the lines of two-way communication.

In addition, exploring the psychological concept of projection can also be instrumental. Research in psychology highlights how individuals may project their own unacknowledged feelings onto their partners, creating a correspondence between inner emotional views and their external relationship.

Practices/Techniques/Exercises for Pattern Recognition

Timeline Analysis

- ❖ Creating a timeline of significant events in your relationship helps you identify patterns over time, offering you a comprehensive view of the correspondence between internal and external experiences.

- ❖ Conduct regular communication reviews where you and your partner evaluate the tone, content, and patterns of your interactions. Recognizing how your internal state(s) may be manifesting in your communication styles demonstrates a good application and understanding of the law of correspondence.

Navigating Transformative Reflections

- ❖ Empower yourself with techniques for conscious pattern-shifting. By identifying undesired patterns and intentionally choosing alternative responses, you can reshape the reflective dynamics within your relationship.

- ❖ Facilitate the development of collaborative growth plans. You and your partner can work together to set shared goals based on recognizing patterns and promoting a collective commitment to transformative change.

Set aside dedicated time to reflect on your interactions, communication styles, and emotional responses within the relationship to examine recurring themes or conflicts so that you recognize the underlying dynamics and any beliefs that may be influencing your interactions. Journaling can be a helpful companion practice for this process.

Lastly, symbols and synchronicities serve as a language through which the universe communicates, reflecting the principles of the Law of Correspondence. By paying attention to these subtle messages can provide guidance and insight into exploring recurring symbols or themes within your relationship, seeking connections between these symbols and your own experiences.

The Law of Correspondence is similar to personal alchemy, transforming challenges into opportunities for growth. By recognizing the correspondence between inner patterns and outer experiences, you engage in a process that elevates consciousness. This process involves cultivating self-awareness, exploring recurring patterns, and embracing the symbolic language of the universe.

As you excitingly continue on your personal journey of manifesting your desired relationship, you are guaranteed to open doors to profound self-awareness and relational evolution. By unraveling the details of how your internal views mirror your shared relationship space, you claim your power to consciously change and shape the narrative of your connection.

∞∞∞

THE LAW OF CORRESPONDENCE

As you grasp the Law of Correspondence, you control the paintbrush for your relationship painting. You can consciously shape the energies that define your shared reality through self-discovery and intentionality.

Shaping Your Vibrations with Intention

Visualization Practices

- ❖ Incorporate visualization exercises where partners envision the desired state of their relationship. This technique helps align individual and shared energies, fostering a harmonious correspondence between aspirations and realities.

Vision Boarding for Couples

- ❖ Partners engage in co-creating a shared vision board that captures their aspirations for the relationship. This visual representation becomes a powerful tool for aligning their energies and desires by positive correspondences.

Affirmation Practices

- ❖ The use of positive affirmations within the relationship. Partners can collaboratively develop affirmations that resonate with their shared goals, amplifying the vibrational frequencies and encouraging a positive atmosphere. Also, see our E-book *Embracing Love Through Denials and Affirmations* at legendaryrelationship.com/love.

Empathetic Listening Techniques

- ❖ Tools for empathetic listening (as stated above) allow partners to deeply understand each other's perspectives. The art of listening becomes a key tool for crafting positive correspondences to adopt mutual understanding and connection.

Nonviolent Communication Strategies

- ❖ The principles of nonviolent communication are utilized by language that promotes empathy and understanding, and couples can transform their verbal exchanges into positive correspondences, nurturing a communication environment—Reframe from elevated emotions and speech in expressing and conveying issues.

Gratitude Practices

- ❖ Cultivate a habit of expressing gratitude within the relationship. Daily or weekly gratitude practices create a positive correspondence loop, amplifying appreciation for each other and contributing to an uplifting relational atmosphere.

Mindfulness and Meditation Together

- ❖ Incorporate mindfulness and meditation practices as shared activities. These tools not only enhance individual well-being but also create a collective space for positive correspondence to flourish.

THE LAW OF CORRESPONDENCE

"It is not a lack of love, but a lack of friendship that makes unhappy marriages." - Friedrich Nietzsche.

Nietzsche's perspective becomes an expressive lens through which we view the Law of Correspondence. It invites you to explore the nuanced connections between different facets of your relationship, emphasizing the importance of friendship as a foundational correspondence that can influence a partnership's overall health and happiness.

Shared story

Meet David and Jackie, a couple who founded their partnership on love and friendship. They were deeply in love yet grappling with the complexities of a long-term and busy relationship. Occasionally, their behavior unintentionally showed that they took their relationship for granted by prioritizing other commitments over their time together. Both balanced demanding careers and extracurricular activities that often kept them apart for days or weeks. While they supported each other, David had been feeling lonely and unprioritized by Jackie. He struggled to express his feelings without seeming selfish or unreasonable. Meanwhile, Jackie, preoccupied with deadlines and constant crises, remained unaware of David's feelings.

Reflective issues began to surface in their relationship, causing conflict and disharmony. David, unsure of how to communicate his feelings, started to exhibit anger and distance. He began entertaining thoughts of being unappreciated and lonely. His attempts to effectively express his needs and wants led to unfavorable behavior and feelings of resentment and loneliness.

It wasn't until they enrolled in a couples' relationship course that the underlying issues became apparent. Their awareness of their lack of quality time and genuine love for each other led them to incorporate suggested couple practices and techniques to enhance quality time and gain a newfound connection.

They incorporated the skills they learned from Legendary Relationship's premium course, "Elevate Your Marriage: Transformational Relationship Course," into their daily lives to address their issues. By doing so, they consciously created positive interactions reflecting both their inner and outer experiences. This intentional approach promoted empathic listening and helped them attune to each other's needs, ensuring both partners always felt valued, loved, and appreciated. As a result, David and Jackie continued to develop and transform their relationship, strengthening their emotional intimacy and lasting joy. Visit our website, legendaryrelationship.com, for enrollment options.

Using the tools outlined in this chapter to create positive correspondence, you and your partner become the artists of your relational reality. By combining intention and conscious creation into the dynamics governed by the Law of Correspondence, you successfully contribute to your desired relationship plan.

By incorporating the Law of Correspondence in your relationship, you can enhance depth, longevity, and mutual satisfaction within your sacred bond of marriage or intimate connection. You gain an appreciation for your relational dynamics and align your actions with principles of synchronization and

THE LAW OF CORRESPONDENCE

balance. Through utilizing tools such as self-reflection, journaling, communication, therapeutic techniques, attachment styles, mindfulness practices, and feedback, you can identify and understand relational patterns, develop a deeper connection, and experience a more enlightened and connected union.

In *What We Believe* by Don Nedd and commentary by Helen W. Carry ©1990, pg5, the concept of correspondence is reflected in the following statement, "We believe with Jesus that our experiences are the reflections of our beliefs and therefore the key to happy and successful living is right thinking followed by right action."

Chapter Five
THE LAW OF CAUSE AND EFFECT
How Actions Contribute to the
Overall Energy of a Relationship

The Law of Cause and Effect, often referred to as karma, asserts that every action you take has a corresponding consequence that influences the quality and trajectory of your connection. It suggests that every action produces an equivalent reaction. This law emphasizes the accountability and responsibility inherent in the choices you make. Similarly, your choices send energetic waves into the universe, creating a universal resound that eventually returns to you in accordance with its original energetic wave.

This chapter coincides with the previous chapter on correspondence, asking you to reflect on the patterns and dynamics present in your relationship. By examining the recurring themes, conflicts, or challenges, you can recognize the underlying causes and identify opportunities for growth and healing. This self-awareness allows you to break free from harmful patterns and cultivate healthier ways of relating to yourself and your partner.

Understanding the Law of Cause and Effect is essential for acquiring a healthy, corresponding relationship filled with mutual respect, trust, and love. As it governs the complex dynamics of your partnership, gaining awareness of the consequences of your actions empowers you to make intentional choices that shape the quality of your connections.

Every positive or negative interaction leaves an imprint on your relationship, influencing your level of intimacy, trust, and emotional safety. Positive actions, such as acts of kindness, support, and empathy, strengthen your bond, encouraging feelings of closeness and connection. Likewise, adverse actions, such as criticism, dishonesty, or neglect, can erode trust, create distance, and lead to resentment and constant conflict.

The Law of Cause and Effect stresses the significance of intentionality in your interactions with your partner. It prompts you to consider the motives behind your actions and their potential consequences on your relationship. By acting with mindfulness and empathy, you consider your partner's needs, emotions, and perspectives, creating mutual respect and reciprocity within your relationship. When you disregard your partner's feelings and emotions regarding your actions, the relationship takes a hit that may or may not be reconcilable. There are consequences to every action you take, and being mindful helps you to make overall decisions that won't negatively impact your relationship.

This law is a directional principle to develop a conscious, compassionate relationship built on authenticity, accountability, and mutual support. It helps you realize that every action you take will have a corresponding consequence and influences the overall energy and atmosphere of your connection with your partner. In essence, your actions serve as the building blocks that shape the value and path or contribute to the destruction of your relationship.

∞∞∞

This law teaches that every action triggers a reaction, and every cause produces an effect. Within your relationship, it informs you that your choices and actions contribute to the overall performance and makeup of the union. Identifying the connected nature of all your actions and consequences gives way to personal responsibility and mindfulness in your interactions. The law wants you to take ownership of your actions and gain an awareness to pause, reflect, and consider potential outcomes before reacting impulsively.

This understanding opens the door to being proactive in problem-solving and conflict resolution by addressing root causes rather than assigning blame. Instead of dwelling on resentment when faced with challenges, you focus on identifying the issues and collaboratively finding solutions. Intentionality becomes paramount in learning to shift and approach your interactions with sincerity, empathy, and respect. That leads to fewer misunderstandings and more favorable outcomes, helping you emerge more unified as a couple.

Studies on social influence reveal how you and your partner subtly influence each other's behaviors. Your actions within your relationship significantly shape its overall energy, contributing to positive or negative dynamics. Research on reciprocity, where partners respond to positive actions (energy) with positive actions (energy) and negative actions (energy) with negative actions (energy), stresses the balance in the give-and-take of relational interactions.

THE LAW OF CAUSE AND EFFECT

Positive actions like gratitude, compassion, and appreciation can increase warmth, trust, and value. Expressing gratitude for your partner's efforts or offering support during tough times advocates feelings of validation and thankfulness.

However, on the other hand, negative actions such as criticism, dishonesty, or neglect create tension, resentment, and distance. They weaken your foundation, erode trust, undermine intimacy, and contribute to you unconsciously having a toxic atmosphere.

Ignoring needs or disrespecting one another damages your emotional connection and leads to hurt and disconnection. Hurt and disconnection become evident through defensiveness, withdrawal, or ongoing dissatisfaction and unhappiness. Being able to see these signs for what they are helps you to consciously start the process of dismantling them.

If you intend to have a loving, respectful, and caring relationship, avoiding negative behavior, actions, and words can have a tremendous impact. Be mindful of your actions and how they affect your partner. Avoidance doesn't eliminate problems; it strengthens and compounds them. Intentionally address and correct issues immediately to eliminate future conflicts and disconnection. Otherwise, they will show up in your relationship in various negative ways.

When you consciously apply this law to your relationship, you can enthusiastically promote growth and shape its momentum. Shifting your perspective to view setbacks or adversity as opportunities for personal and relational development prepares you to avoid or navigate challenges more effectively.

However, your actions' cumulative effect dramatically influences the relationship's energy and resiliency. Deliberately choosing positive behaviors over the smallest negative ones contributes to a supportive and loving partnership. When you prioritize the actions in your relationship, you create an environment where both of you feel valued and cherished, enriching the partnership.

∞∞∞

This principle reminds you to explore the potential of embracing responsibility for your relationship's positive and challenging aspects. The Law of Cause and Effect encourages you to become aware of your personal responsibility in your relationship, acknowledging your power over your choices and actions.

Recognizing your role ensures that you take ownership of your actions and their impact on your partner. This awareness gives you a sense of accountability, helping you avoid blaming your partner for issues you might have contributed to. When you acknowledge your influence, you can better identify areas to improve, leading to personal growth and a healthier relationship dynamic.

Understand your power to influence the course of your relationship through your thoughts, words, and actions. Your choices and behaviors have a direct impact on the emotional climate. By acknowledging your behavior, you take ownership of your role as an active participant in the co-creation of the relationship.

THE LAW OF CAUSE AND EFFECT

Taking ownership of your actions entails accepting accountability for the consequences they generate. Whether positive or negative, your behaviors imprint on the relational terrain. It involves being honest with yourself and your partner about the impact of your actions and being willing to take responsibility for any harm caused. Owning your actions supports transparency, trust, and integrity within the relationship.

Awareness of your responsibility empowers you to make conscious and deliberate choices. This empowerment means you can actively work towards resolving conflicts, enhancing communication, and building a stronger bond. Instead of feeling helpless or reactive in the relationship, you understand that you have the authority to shape its course through your actions and decisions, irrespective of your partners.

Personal responsibility also encompasses honoring the commitments and agreements you make within your relationship. This includes major agreements like fidelity and support and minor agreements such as household chores or spending quality time together. It also includes upholding promises, being reliable and trustworthy, and respecting your partner's boundaries and needs. Consistently upholding your commitments demonstrates reliability, respect, and dedication to the partnership.

Moreover, this awareness promotes mutual respect and trust. When both partners recognize and accept their responsibilities, it creates a balanced and equitable environment. It shows that you value your partner's feelings and perspectives through self-awareness.

MANIFEST A JOY-FILLED RELATIONSHIP

Developing self-awareness is crucial for understanding how your thoughts, emotions, and behaviors shape and contribute to the overall health of your partnership. It involves a willingness to examine your own motivations, biases, beliefs, values, triggers, and patterns of interaction. By practicing self-awareness, you can see how your actions impact your partner and the relationship.

Acknowledging your power over your choices helps prevent feelings of resentment and frustration. Taking responsibility makes you less likely to feel victimized or controlled by circumstances and more likely to feel satisfied and fulfilled in the relationship. It allows you to approach challenges proactively, seeking solutions rather than dwelling on problems.

Personal relationship responsibility entails responding to challenges and conflicts with mindfulness and intentionality. Instead of reacting impulsively based on emotions or past conditioning, it involves pausing to consider your actions' potential consequences. Empathy, compassion, and a commitment to finding mutually beneficial solutions characterize mindful responses.

The concept of personal responsibility in your relationship invites you to engage in ongoing self-examination and open and honest dialogue about your roles and responsibilities in the partnership. It requires you to confront uncomfortable truths, acknowledge areas for growth, and make proactive changes. By embracing personal responsibility, you lay the foundation for a relationship characterized by trust and authenticity built on shared empowerment and overall satisfaction.

THE LAW OF CAUSE AND EFFECT

Remember, it's your repetitive choices and their immediate and lasting consequences that shape your life. Whether immediate or in the future, it's the thinking and emotions behind your choices that matter. Becoming aware of why and how you make relationship decisions is crucial because we often focus on our partner's actions and judge them as right or wrong.

Today, as you read, shift your focus away from your partner's behaviors and concentrate on yourself and what you can do to become more self-aware for positive self-development. Self-development is a continuous process achieved through truthful self-reflection. The benefits of this self-development far outweigh any difficulties you might face now or in the future.

Self-reflection becomes a top priority in manifesting. It involves introspection and a sincere evaluation of your views, actions, and reactions. By examining your motives, patterns, and reactions, you gain awareness of how your actions affect your partner and the relationship as a whole. As you adopt mindfulness practices, you'll notice its enhancing effects in all areas of your life. Mindfulness entails being fully present in the moment by observing your thoughts and emotions without judgment and developing awareness of your actions (negative and positive) and their consequences. By staying mindful in your interactions with your partner, you can make more intentional choices and respond thoughtfully rather than reactively, laying the groundwork for effective communication, positive actions, and reciprocity. This will help you switch from a state of reaction to a state of consciously choosing thoughts, emotions, actions, and behaviors that will positively affect every area of your life and help create a cycle of goodwill that returns to you in various forms within your relationship.

As you grow in consciousness, you will be able to recognize and lessen the inevitability of unintended consequences, in turn learning how to overcome challenges and transform seemingly adverse outcomes into learning opportunities. Utilizing reflective practices, such as journaling and post-event analysis, provides you with tools to process your experiences and extract valuable lessons from them. By engaging in self-reflection and approaching challenges with a growth-oriented mindset, you can shift your perspective and leverage the Law of Cause and Effect as a catalyst for personal and relational development.

"The best way to predict the future is to create it." - Peter Drucker

Drucker's perspective should become your guiding principle as you study the Law of Cause and Effect. It challenges you to approach your relationship proactively, recognizing that your choices today contribute to the relational model you shape tomorrow. By understanding the domino effects of your actions, you can intentionally craft positive narratives and co-create positive dynamics within your connection. Take responsibility, and let your crafting begin!

∞∞∞

One of the critical tools for accountability and growth through self-reflection is journaling. Keeping a journal allows you to document your experiences, emotions, and reactions privately and non-judgmentally. Writing down your thoughts and feelings can help you gain clarity, identify unhealthy patterns, see beyond current appearances, and recognize areas for improvement. And if you have yet to realize it, journaling is a key component in manifesting desires. Therefore, if you are not a journaler, start with 5 to 10 minutes, once or twice a week, and work your way up to increased time until you find what works best for you. Small steps are better than no steps at all. To have something different, you must be willing to do something different.

Another effective tool for accountability and growth is post-event analysis. You reflect on your past interactions or conflicts within the relationship to understand what happened, why it happened, and how you can address it differently in the future. By examining the root causes of your issues and taking responsibility for your role in them, you are better equipped to learn from your mistakes. You can identify areas for progress, implement proactive changes, and make a conscious effort to adjust your behavior where needed.

Listening to constructive feedback, being optimistic, and taking it into account can help you obtain a different viewpoint, ultimately enhancing your self-awareness for furthering personal growth and advancement.

Being responsible for your emotions means recognizing and managing them healthily. This includes avoiding projecting negative emotions onto your partner, taking time to cool down before addressing conflicts, and seeking constructive ways to express yourself without causing harm. Being able to control your emotions and not project them or place blame allows you to stay in control of your feelings and the actions that can have lasting consequences. This emotional control gives you a sense of encouragement and accomplishment over once-challenging situations. It's about taking back your power instead of inadvertently giving it away.

Accepting responsibility for resolving conflicts requires approaching disagreements with openness, empathy, and a willingness to find mutually beneficial solutions. It involves refraining from projecting or defensiveness and instead focusing on understanding your partner's perspective and working together to address underlying issues.

Accepting personal responsibility also entails a commitment to continuous self-improvement and growth. It involves recognizing that you are imperfect and that there is always room for learning and development. By actively seeking opportunities for growth and reflecting on your experiences, you can become a more compassionate, empathetic, and resilient partner.

Understanding the Law of Cause and Effect requires a heightened awareness of one's choices. Conscious choices, fueled by positive intentions, create an effect of harmonious consequences. Nevertheless, conscious decisions, driven by harmful intentions, create an effect of inharmonious consequences.

Just as a gardener sows seeds in fertile soil, your intentional actions become seeds planted in the universal soil, influencing the quality of the experiences that bloom in your life. Therefore, we suggest you consciously consider your actions and true intentions before sending them into the ether. There is a saying we use in technology about the data users input into databases – "Garbage in, garbage out!" If you put garbage into the ethers, you'll know what to expect.

THE LAW OF CAUSE AND EFFECT

∞∞∞

This law emphasizes the principles of responsibility and accountability. Every choice you make carries consequences, and acknowledging this truth allows you to take ownership of your actions. Like a sculptor shaping a piece of clay, the hands guiding the creation are responsible. Similarly, you, and only you, shape your destinies through the sculpting power of your choices, and embracing accountability ensures that you employ this power with conscious intent and not with the flame of blame.

Within your relationship, personal responsibility can manifest in some of the various ways.

Accountability - Taking ownership of your actions involves recognizing when you've made mistakes or unintentionally created negative reactions, acknowledging their impact, and being willing to address and rectify them without deflection. This requires humility, honesty, and a commitment to making amends, when necessary, regardless of the issue.

Communication - Being responsible in communication entails expressing yourself authentically and respectfully, actively listening to your partner's perspectives, and considering their feelings and needs. Effective communication nurtures understanding, trust, and connection.

Boundaries - Setting and respecting boundaries are critical aspects of personal responsibility. It involves understanding your limits, communicating them to your partner, and honoring their boundaries. Healthy boundaries create a sense of safety and autonomy within your relationship. Establishing clear boundaries leaves little room for errors and guessing.

Conscious Co-Creation - At the heart of the Law of Cause and Effect is conscious co-creation. As co-creators of your relationship, you and your partner must recognize the impact of your thoughts, words, and actions. Understand the importance of intentional choices in promoting a positive and thriving relationship. The practical exercises and self-reflection prompts in this book help you become mindful architects of what you are building as your shared reality.

The Principle of Reciprocity - Operating on reciprocity, the Law of Cause and Effect stresses that the energy you emit into the universe - positive or negative - eventually returns to you. Visualize a boomerang hurled into the sky; it inevitably returns to its originator. Similarly, your thoughts, feelings, and actions act as energetic boomerangs, guided by your invisible energy to go out into the universe and circle back to you - its originator – bringing back – the same invisible energy in which it was sent out.

Breaking the Cycle - The Law of Cause and Effect invites you to break free from cyclical negative karma patterns. Suppose you are always entangled in unfavorable circumstances. In that case, this law encourages the Big I and the Three C's - introspection and conscious course correction. Imagine a ship navigating choppy waters; adjusting its course ensures a smoother

THE LAW OF CAUSE AND EFFECT

voyage. Similarly, by identifying the sources of challenges and making deliberate choices to redirect your energy, you can best alter the path of your experiences.

Healing and Growth Through Reflection - Reflection involves taking a step back from the immediate situation and uncovering the underlying emotions and motivations. It's about creating a safe space where you and your partner can explore your thoughts and feelings. By setting aside dedicated time for reflection together, you can create an environment where both of you are comfortable identifying issues and working together to resolve them in healthier ways.

∞∞∞

Every action, word, and gesture play a part in shaping the dynamics between you and your partner. Therefore, positive causation involves intentionally developing behaviors and attitudes that contribute to and align with growth, happiness, and harmony.

Clear and truthful communication forms the foundation of a healthy relationship. It's about having a noncontroversial and supportive environment where both partners feel comfortable expressing their thoughts, feelings, and needs without fear of judgment or criticism.

A healthy relationship is one where both partners feel heard, understood, and valued. Practicing active listening is vital. Prioritize active listening by fully engaging with your partner's perspective and validating their experiences. Understand that everyone's point is valid. Please take the time to see your partner's point of view and valid concerns. This allows you to be open to another perspective, not right or wrong, but just other possibilities and views.

Engaging and practicing empathy shows your partner that you are willing to put yourself in their shoes and truly seek to understand their feelings and needs. You are creating a space to communicate your thoughts and emotions candidly by using "I" statements to express yourself without blaming or accusing your partner. Regularly check in with each other to ensure that you keep the established lines of communication open and address any issues promptly and constructively.

Empathy is fundamental to reinforcing your foundation of emotional connection and intimacy. Empathy is the ability to understand and share in your partner's feelings. Building empathy in your relationship entails understanding your partner's experiences, perspectives, and emotions and, in turn, responding maturely with compassion and understanding, putting yourself in their shoes, seeking to empathize with their joys, struggles, and challenges and validating their feelings and experiences, even if you disagree with them. You can work on showing empathy through small gestures of kindness, such as listening openly, providing emotional support, giving comfort, encouraging words, or expressing appreciation. Practicing empathy and understanding strengthens the bond of trust, mutual respect, and gratitude. You are demonstrating to your mate your willingness to work on the relationship and incorporate new habits and behaviors starting with you.

Just as empathy reinforces your foundation, respect cements the foundation upon which you build healthy relationships. Treating your partner with kindness, consideration, and dignity, even during disagreements or conflicts, establishes an environment of respect. Start small by encouraging a sense of equality and trust by valuing your partner's opinions, perspectives, and boundaries, and at all costs, refrain from belittling, criticizing, or dismissing them – especially in public or around friends. If you believe something needs addressing, wait until you are alone to express your feelings and thoughts respectfully and dignifiedly.

Begin practicing and expressing gratitude and appreciation for your partner regularly by making it a habit to acknowledge their contributions, strengths, and efforts. Remember that you are forming new patterns and behaviors relating to your partner, so keep accentuating the positive and eliminating the negative. Celebrating their successes and achievements, no matter how small, and affirming your belief in their abilities and worth shows your unconditional support of them and the relationship. This opens the door of reciprocity and enhances the overall satisfaction and happiness you feel within your relationship.

Spending quality time together is essential for nurturing intimacy, connection, and emotional bonds and consciously prioritizing dedicated time for sharing activities, conversations, and fun experiences. Take time out to create rituals and routines that allow you to connect on a deeper level, such as regular date nights, morning walks, exercising, bike rides, or shared hobbies. Or even deliberately making time for little things each partner values, like cooking dinner together, buying treats and popping popcorn for movie night, or simply cuddling on the couch and making lasting, bond-forming memories together. Disconnect from distractions and devices during your time together, allowing you to focus entirely on each other and strengthen your emotional connection. Use this time to laugh, play, and create cherished memories that deepen your bond and reinforce your commitment to each other. Don't use this time to discuss issues; make this about creating a new space for each other first. Once you have established spending more quality time together to strengthen your bond, it will open up opportunities for enhancing practical communication skills to resolve old conflicts – if they still exist.

Conflicts and misunderstandings are inevitable in any relationship, but how you handle them can make all the difference to the overall health of your relationship. Practicing forgiveness frees you from the feeling and belief of injustice or hurt. "Charles Fillmore, in The Revealing Word, defines forgiveness as 'A process of giving up the false for the true;... and true forgiveness is only established through renewing the mind and body with thoughts and words of Truth.'"

Learning to release and let go of resentments, grudges, and past grievances that weigh you down and hinder your ability to move forward is crucial in manifesting something joyous and loving. Working with the ability to forgive quickly and without reservation allows you and your partner to move forward with a clean slate. Approach conflicts with a willingness to understand, forgive, and reconcile rather than seeking to assign blame or win arguments. Communicate promptly and constructively about your feelings, needs, and concerns, and work together to find mutually acceptable solutions. Present your concerns by stating accurate things that cannot be debated; avoid guessing, blaming, hypotheticals, or destructive words.

By practicing forgiveness and letting go, you intentionally create a safe space for healing, growth, communication, and rebirth.

Setting and pursuing shared goals as a couple can be a powerful way to mend separateness and disconnectedness. Welcoming new practices and routines in working together to identify common interests, values, and aspirations and then create actionable plans to achieve them allows you and your partner to contribute to the relationship's vision by each of you feeling heard, valued, and appreciated. Pursuing those shared goals together not only strengthens the sense of partnership and teamwork but also provides opportunities for growth and mutual support, rebuilding areas of your relationship that may need repair.

Two individuals committed to their own personal growth and development, as well as the growth and development of the relationship, comprise healthy relationships. You can encourage yourself and your partner to pursue your passions, interests, and goals. Supporting each other's journey of self-discovery and self-improvement acquires a higher sense of value and appreciation, which positively reflects back in the relationship. Take time for self-care and self-reflection, pouring into your physical, emotional, and spiritual well-being. Set personal goals and aspirations by working together to create a shared vision for your future. Working on individual growth and development will bring vitality, fulfillment, and purpose to your relationship, restructuring and enriching the bond you share with your partner.

Adopting positive causation in your relationship requires intentional effort and commitment from both partners. Incorporating these practical steps into your relationship can create a loving, supportive, and fulfilling partnership. By encouraging open communication, empathy, mutual respect, quality time together, forgiveness, and individual growth, you lay the groundwork for your relationship to thrive and flourish, even in the face of challenges, differences, and adversity.

∞∞∞

When you combine positive intentions and positive actions in your relationship dynamics, they will have tremendously positive effects in all areas of your life. Because of your newly developed actions and practices, those effects will effectively contribute to your relationship's positive feedback loop, reinforcing feelings of love, security, and satisfaction between you and your partner. Nonetheless, as you consistently engage in the habit of acts of kindness and support, your relational atmosphere transforms and becomes more conducive to growth, connection, understanding, and intimacy.

Regarding the Law of Cause and Effect within your relationship, it's essential to understand the profound effects that positive actions can have on your relationship dynamics. Numerous studies and research findings support the idea that small acts of kindness and positivity can significantly improve relationship satisfaction and overall well-being.

Studies in social psychology have demonstrated that positive actions - such as expressing gratitude or showing empathy - can strengthen the emotional bond between partners and enhance overall relationship satisfaction. For example, a study published in the Journal of Personality and Social Psychology found that couples who regularly express gratitude toward each other experience higher levels of relationship quality and commitment.

Consider the "Love Lab" experiments by Dr. John Gottman and his team, where they observed couples interacting in a controlled environment to understand the dynamics of healthy relationships. Their research revealed that couples who consistently engaged in positive behaviors, such as expressing appreciation, showing affection, and practicing empathy, had more robust and more resilient relationships over time. Another study published in the Journal of Marriage and Family discovered that couples who regularly engage in acts of kindness towards each other reported higher levels of marital happiness and lower levels of conflict.

Positive actions within a relationship create an effect that extends far beyond the initial time and space. When one partner engages in acts of kindness, support, and affection, it sets off a chain reaction of positive responses and reactions from their partner. This creates positive reactions within the relationship, reinforcing feelings of love, trust, and connection.

For example, when one partner expresses gratitude for their partner's efforts or shows appreciation for their presence, it fosters a sense of validation and warmth within the relationship. This simple act of kindness can lead to increased feelings of closeness and intimacy.

Books like *The Five Love Languages* by Dr. Gary Chapman also emphasize the importance of expressing love and appreciation in ways that resonate with your partner. By understanding and speaking your partner's love language, whether through words of affirmation, acts of service, quality time, physical touch, or receiving gifts, you can strengthen the emotional connection and deepen your bond.

Knowing that in every relationship, there are going to be ups and downs, and one famous ending to that statement has been - but it's the dedication and commitment to each other that make it work; reminds us of the enduring power of positivity and commitment in relationships. By consistently nurturing your relationship with acts of love, kindness, and dedication, you can weather any storm.

Furthermore, positive actions within a relationship can have a positive effect on other aspects of the partnership. When one partner demonstrates empathy and understanding during conflict or disagreement, it paves the way for productive communication and conflict resolution. This can lead to greater harmony and cooperation, creating a supportive and nurturing environment for both partners.

Moreover, the effects of positive actions extend beyond the relationship itself and can impact other areas of partners' lives. For example, studies have shown that when partners feel loved and supported within their relationship, they are more likely to experience greater overall well-being and satisfaction in other areas of their lives, such as their career, health, and personal development.

Practical exercises and tools, such as gratitude journaling, daily affirmations, and random acts of kindness, can help you incorporate positive actions into your daily interactions with your partner. Take time each day to reflect on and express gratitude for your partner's presence in your life and look for opportunities to surprise them with gestures of love and affection.

Some suggestions could be to incorporate tools like the "appreciation jar" which can be beneficial by leaving little notes of appreciation in a jar to enhance feelings of love. This is done by setting aside a jar and periodically dropping in a note of appreciation for each other's kindness, support, or love. Take turns reading the notes aloud to each other whenever you need a reminder of the positive impact you have on each other's lives. Or try keeping a gratitude journal where you jot down three things you appreciate about your partner each day. You can share the entries or keep them to yourself to read later as a reminder of the qualities you admire and appreciate in your partner.

Practice empathy by putting yourself in your partner's shoes. If you currently struggle with empathy, take time for yourself to work on this area. Spend intentional time seeing things from your mate's perspective, as well as considering other alternative points of view. You'll be better prepared to act and react with empathy and kindness when situations arise. This strengthens your connection and earns you brownie points because your partner won't expect it.

Understanding the effects of positive actions on relationship dynamics can empower you to grow a more loving, supportive, and fulfilling partnership with your significant other. By consciously incorporating kindness, compassion, and appreciation into your daily interactions, you are putting in place all the things necessary to manifest a happy and joy-filled relationship.

When you apply positive actions to your relationship dynamics and incorporate beneficial exercises, tools, and techniques into your relationship, you can create and sustain a warm and supportive environment where love and happiness thrive.

Research on the "broaden-and-build" theory suggests that positive emotions, such as love, gratitude, and joy, broaden our perspective and build psychological resources that enhance resilience and well-being. When you apply this theory to your relationship, positive actions not only strengthen the bond between you and your partner but also create a basin of positive emotions that buffer against stress and adversity.

In addition, exploring literature on relationships provides invaluable insights into the power of positive actions. Authors like John Gottman, in his book *The Seven Principles for Making Marriage Work*, emphasize the importance of cultivating a culture of appreciation and fondness in relationships. Similarly, Maya Angelou's quote, "I've learned that people will forget what you said, people will forget what you did, but people will never forget how you made them feel," accentuates the lasting impact of positive actions on relationship dynamics.

Another straightforward and adequate exercise is the "gratitude letter," where you and your partner write a letter to one another expressing your gratitude for specific acts of kindness, support, or positive character traits. Schedule a date night, movie night, or dedicated quality time together and share your letters. Take turns reading your letters without disruption or commenting. Refrain from condemnation or unhealthy joking and sarcasm. By having each other's full attention and time, discussing your letters will build connection, empathy, gratitude, joy, love, appreciation, and a host of other positive deposits into your relationship account.

Another technique is "active constructive responding," where you actively engage and respond enthusiastically to your partner's good news or positive experiences. Try this without making your partner aware of what you are doing and watching their initial response. Keep incorporating it into your daily practice until it becomes a habit, and the law of reciprocity will have you both sharing and supporting each other enthusiastically. This physical display of love and support will benefit all areas of your relationship.

Additionally, positive actions within a relationship can inspire reciprocal behavior from partners, leading to a cycle of positivity and growth. When one partner goes out of their way to make their partner feel unique or valued, it often motivates the other partner to do the same in return. This reciprocal exchange of positive actions strengthens the emotional connection between partners. It fosters a sense of mutual support and appreciation.

The cumulative effect of consistent positive actions over time cannot be overstated. Just as negative actions can erode trust and intimacy, positive actions build a strong foundation of love, respect, and mutual support that sustains the relationship through challenges and hardships.

Experiencing the effects of positive actions in your relationship dynamics enables you to nurture a loving and fulfilling partnership. By actively and intentionally prioritizing kindness, appreciation, and empathy in your daily interactions, you can create a relationship that thrives on positivity, support, and resiliency.

Positive actions, such as expressions of love, appreciation, and support, serve as building blocks for emotional intimacy within your relationship. When you consistently engage in those behaviors, you create an inlet of positive emotions and emotional closeness. This emotional closeness forms the foundation of a healthy and fulfilling relationship, enhancing your overall satisfaction and longevity.

Positive actions contribute to constructive communication patterns. When you express appreciation, actively listen to each other, and respond empathetically, you create a supportive space for open dialogue. This encourages honest expression of thoughts and feelings, reduces defensiveness and conflict, and raises understanding and respect. Over time, these positive communication habits strengthen the relationship and promote effective problem-solving and conflict resolution.

When you demonstrate reliability, loyalty, and commitment through your actions, you instill confidence in each other and strengthen the foundation of trust. This trust forms the basis of a secure attachment bond, allowing you to feel comfortable being vulnerable and authentic with each other. As a result, your relationship becomes a source of comfort and support, enhancing your overall satisfaction and well-being.

The effects of positive actions extend to individual growth and development. When you experience love, appreciation, and encouragement from each other, you feel empowered to pursue personal goals and aspirations. This mutual support fosters a sense of self-esteem and self-efficacy, enabling you to thrive both personally and interpersonally. As you continue to grow and evolve together, your relationship becomes a dynamic and enriching journey of mutual growth and fulfillment.

THE LAW OF CAUSE AND EFFECT

In essence, the effects of positive actions on relationship dynamics are profound and far-reaching. By having a culture of kindness, appreciation, and support within your partnership, you can establish a relationship that thrives on emotional connection, effective communication, trust, and personal growth. As these positive behaviors become ingrained in the very being of your relationship, they create a solid and resilient bond that withstands the test of time.

Practices/Techniques/Exercises

Gratitude Journaling - Each evening, take a few minutes to write down three things you appreciate about your partner. Research shows gratitude journaling increases relationship satisfaction and fosters emotional intimacy.

Random Acts of Kindness - Surprise your partner with small acts of kindness, such as making their favorite meal or leaving love notes around the house. Research suggests that performing acts of kindness increases feelings of happiness and strengthens relationship bonds.

Appreciation Jar - Set up an easily accessible jar and label it "Appreciation Jar" where you and your partner can write notes of appreciation for each other's actions and qualities. Regularly read these notes together to reinforce positive feelings and deepen your connection.

Love Languages Assessment - Take the Love Languages quiz together to understand each other's preferred ways of giving and receiving love. This tool helps you tailor your expressions of affection to better resonate with your partner's needs.

MANIFEST A JOY-FILLED RELATIONSHIP

Practice active listening by fully focusing on what your partner is saying without interrupting or judging. Use reflective listening techniques to validate their emotions and show empathy.

Make it a habit to express gratitude to your partner every day for something they've done or a quality you admire. Research shows that expressing gratitude strengthens relationship satisfaction and fosters long-term commitment.

Studies have found that expressing gratitude towards your partner leads to higher relationship satisfaction and increased feelings of closeness and connection.

Small acts of kindness and generosity contribute significantly to relationship quality and marital stability.

Active listening fosters emotional intimacy and strengthens communication within relationships, leading to greater relationship satisfaction and lower conflict levels.

Incorporating these exercises, tools, and techniques into your relationship underscores the impact of positive actions on your relationship dynamics within your marriage or intimate partnership. You can mindfully create a culture of kindness, support, and love within your relationship, leading to greater happiness, fulfillment, and resilience. By embracing the power of positive actions, you are in full control of creating rippling effects of positivity that extend far beyond your relationship, enriching your life and the lives of those around you.

THE LAW OF CAUSE AND EFFECT

In 'What We Believe' by Don Nedd and commentary by Helen W. Carry ©1990, pg2, the concept that each person creates their own experiences: "For too long, people have believed that the negative conditions that come into their lives do so because it is God's will; or that God is punishing them for some wrong they may have done. We must come into the realization that God's nature is absolute good and HE cannot will anything other than His nature. Therefore, God wills good and only good for His children - that includes love, joy, peace, happiness and all that is desired for a prosperous life..."

Chapter Six
THE LAW OF ATTRACTION
Attraction in Action in Relationships

Have you ever heard of the Law of Attraction? Of course, you have. One of the most widely known and transformative laws, the Law of Attraction, states that like attracts like. Have you wondered how it applies to your relationship? This chapter reveals that the true essence of the Law of Attraction is the power of your thoughts, emotions, and beliefs in shaping your reality. By aligning your inner world with your desires, you learn to attract positive experiences and consciously manifest the relationship you envision. Is it simple, yes; is it easy, no!

The Law of Attraction suggests that like attracts like, both in thought and emotion. Choosing positive thoughts and feelings creates an attraction where more positive experiences will come into your life and relationship. Where dwelling on negativity may bring about undesirable circumstances and discord. Did you know that at the nucleus of the Law of Attraction is the understanding that your thoughts and emotions not only influence your individual experiences but also contribute to the collective energetic field of the universe?

Fueled by intentional focus on creating positive thoughts and emotions, this collective consciousness causes a vibrational effect, elevating the vibrational frequency of the entire interconnected universe. When you choose positivity, you contribute to this uplifting energy, enhancing your life and those around you.

In this chapter, you will travel into the Law of Attraction and see how it influences your relationship. You will gain awareness as to how your thoughts and emotions shape your interactions and experiences with your partner. By understanding and applying this law, you can create your relationship, attract positive experiences, and transform your love life. Are you ready? Then let's go! But first, get comfortable and adjust your lighting as we expose this law and its power in your personal relationship.

∞∞∞

The Law of Attraction has long been regarded as an influential force shaping the course of your life. Its influence on your relationship affects not only your initial attraction but also ongoing attraction. The law reveals its central role in shaping your relationship through the transformative power of your thoughts and feelings. This law suggests that like attracts like, meaning the energy you send out, whether consciously or subconsciously, magnetically draws corresponding energies into your life. This principle serves as the doorway to intentional manifestation, encouraging you to actively co-create your relationship story.

This means that the qualities you embody and the vibrations you send out determine the nature of the connection you form with your partner. Essentially, what you focus on, you attract into your relationship. This applies not only to your thoughts and emotions but also to your actions and experiences.

Realize that attraction transcends mere physicality; it's rooted in energetic significance. Therefore, partners who share vibrational frequencies naturally gravitate toward each other, raising a magnetic pull that goes beyond the visible. Therefore, it attracts you to experiences and circumstances that align with your thoughts, emotions, beliefs, and actions. The Law of Attraction operates on multiple levels in marriage and intimate relationships. It influences your initial attraction to your partner, shaping the compatibility and chemistry that drew you together. Then, it continues to exert its influence throughout your relationship, affecting your quality of communication, emotional quality, and overall accord between you and your partner.

As we move into the Law of Attraction, realize that you are stepping into a state of being where your thoughts and energies with your partner can blend to create amazing lines of connection. By grasping the magnetic forces in action, you can intentionally create a relationship that resonates with your highest visions and aspirations.

Understanding this law involves recognizing that all the energy you release - both positive and negative - about your relationship plays a significant role in shaping your connections with your partner.

Think about it this way: focusing on positive thoughts and emotions makes you more likely to attract positive experiences and emotions into your relationship. Likewise, if you dwell on negativity or harbor feelings of doubt, fear, or resentment, you may unintentionally attract similar energy into your relationship, leading to undesired conflict or dissatisfaction.

But here's the good news: by understanding and utilizing the Law of Attraction, you have the power to shape your relationship in positive ways. It all starts with clarifying your intentions.

Establishing clear and concise intentions regarding your relationship is very important. Each partner should be willing to ask themselves what kind of relationship they want and what qualities they want to develop in their relationship and themselves. These are crucial questions to understanding your path together and devising a plan to get there.

By expressing your goals and aspirations, you align your energies, paving the way for intentional manifestation. This enables both of you to consciously shape the dynamics of your relationship and create a union that embodies all the elements that you foresee. Instead of one that is created through the universal collective consciousness and may be filled with hate, bitterness, misunderstanding, and resentment. When two individuals align their thoughts, emotions, and intentions toward a shared vision, the magnetic pull of their collective energies intensifies, strengthening the synergy between them and the universe.

Once you've identified your desires, the next step is to align your thoughts, emotions, and actions with those intentions. Visualize your ideal relationship, feel the emotions associated with it, and take inspired action toward manifesting it into reality. This might involve having a routine of gratitude, practicing self-love, or engaging in activities that bring you joy and fulfillment.

Remember, the Law of Attraction is not about wishing for something and passively waiting for it to happen. It's about actively creating your reality with the universe by aligning your energy with your desires. In the context of relationships, this means adopting a positive mindset, nurturing loving emotions, and taking intentional steps toward building your fulfilling partnership.

Ultimately, you become an intentional creator of your romantic reality. Tapping into the power of your thoughts and emotions, you shape your relational destiny and gain deep connections rooted in energetic alignment.

So, invite the power of the Law of Attraction, whether you're seeking to attract a new partner or improve your existing relationship. By becoming a conscious and deliberate creator of your romantic reality, you can manifest the love and connection you truly desire. Please don't leave it up to chance. Guide your relationship on the path you wish it to follow and enlist the universe's help.

∞∞∞

The influence of your thoughts and emotions serves as powerful magnets that attract experiences and consequences that resonate with your personal frequency. Therefore, the thoughts you constantly entertain about yourself, your partner, and the dynamics of your connection significantly impact the energy you radiate. Suppose you focus on positive thoughts and emotions such as love, gratitude, and appreciation regardless of what is going on in your relationship. In that case, it will amplify the vibration of harmony and connection, strengthening the bond between you and your partner. If you constantly focus on negative thoughts rooted in fear, jealousy, distrust, doubt, or resentment, you will undoubtedly generate discordant energies that can erode the foundation of your relationship. Recognize what thoughts and emotions you are holding and emitting regarding the entire dynamics of your relationship. That means being aware of your feelings about past issues, careers, time, family dynamics, love, happiness, respect, and life itself. What unconsciously are you attracting into your relationship that you'd rather not experience?

While your thoughts set the foundation, your emotions serve as powerful incentives, giving your intentions a strong, energetic charge that enhances their magnetic pull. Imagine your emotions are like vibrant magnetic fields. Your authentic feelings of gratitude, for example, raise the vibrational frequency of your thoughts, making the magnetic attraction of similar energies stronger in your life. Therefore, the law reminds you to be aware of your emotional states and understand their importance as key factors in the magnetic manifestation process.

During challenging times, your thoughts and emotions emit frequencies that resonate with the universe, attracting similar energies back to you. This means that if you focus on negativity, anger, and complaints, you will inevitably attract more of those experiences into your relationship. The universe doesn't pick and choose; you do.

Consider this: if 90% of your thoughts are negative, your predominant desire is negative, not positive. The universe responds to the dominant frequency you emit, which, in this case, is negativity. As a result, you attract more negative experiences between you and your partner, creating a vicious cycle that can be difficult to break. To change this pattern, you must shift your focus from what you don't want to experience in your relationship to what you do want to experience.

First, become aware of your thoughts and emotions. Pay attention to how you feel and what you usually think about.

If you notice that you're frequently angry, complaining, or harboring negative thoughts, recognize that these are the frequencies you send out into the universe. You must change your internal dialogue to attract positive experiences and improve your relationship. Constant negative thoughts will create negative experiences, however, keeping the same thoughts and wanting a different outcome will not happen.

It is through your thinking that the things in your experience are created. You might even argue that you do think positive thoughts, but you are getting the same results. Those results are the true indications of your inner thoughts and feelings behind all your actions and interactions. The universe does not lie, it creates exactly what you vibrate out. You might not be sold on this truth, but if you have had many negative experiences in the past and you are constantly reminding yourself of those negative experiences you are actually sending out vibrations to get more of those same experiences. That's why it is important to understand how the universe works and how you can consciously work with it, not against it.

Start by focusing on gratitude. Gratitude is one of the many powerful tools in manifesting. Gratitude aids in shifting your frequency from negative to positive. Make it a habit to express gratitude for your partner and your relationship. Even during tough times, find something to be thankful for. This could be as simple as appreciating your partner's smile, their support, or the good times you've shared. By consistently focusing on what you appreciate, you begin to emit a positive frequency that attracts more positive interactions and experiences.

When you genuinely understand the magnetic pull of energies within the Law of Attraction, you will become aware of how much your thoughts act like magnets. When you acknowledge the power of gratitude in intentional manifestation, you realize how it can amplify your attraction. By being grateful for what you have now and what you want in your relationship, you're boosting the positive vibes, drawing more of what you value. Also, when you both make gratitude a habit, you create fertile ground for your shared dreams to come true. By appreciating the blessings and growth in your relationship, you deepen your connection and attract more of these good things into your lives.

Another effective practice is visualization. When you introduce and use visualization techniques in your relationship, you unlock the power of your imagination. Spend time each day seeing and living the kind of relationship you desire using your universal power of mind action. See yourself and your partner happy, loving, and connected. Imagine the seemingly negative things in your relationship as positive experiences you want to create together. The more vividly you can picture these scenarios, the stronger the frequency you emit. This helps align your inner world with your desires, making attracting those experiences into your reality easier. By vividly imagining the ideal state of your partnership, you tap into the power of unformed universal mental energy, projecting your desired reality into physical form.

Affirmations, an additional influential tool, can also significantly influence your frequency. Affirmations are positive, declarative statements you repeat to yourself to influence your subconscious mind. They reinforce a desired belief or outcome, helping shift your mindset and focus toward your goal. Affirmations can be a powerful tool for personal growth and manifestation, as they help reprogram your thinking patterns and align your actions with your goals. Create affirmations that reflect the relationship you want to manifest.

How Affirmations Work

- ❖ Repetition - By consistently repeating affirmations, you embed them into your subconscious mind. This repetition helps replace negative or limiting beliefs with positive, empowering ones.

- ❖ Positive Focus - Affirmations direct your focus towards positive outcomes and possibilities. By concentrating on what you want rather than what you don't want, you align your thoughts and emotions with your desires.

- ❖ Emotional Connection - When you say affirmations with feeling and conviction, they resonate more deeply. Emotions amplify the power of affirmations, making them more effective in influencing your subconscious mind.

- ❖ Visualization - Affirmations often include visualizing the desired outcome. This mental imagery helps create a clear picture of your goals, making them feel more attainable and real.

Benefits of Affirmations

- ❖ Affirmations help build self-confidence and self-esteem by reinforcing positive beliefs about yourself and your abilities.

- ❖ Positive affirmations can counteract negative thoughts and reduce stress and anxiety by promoting a more optimistic outlook.

- ❖ Affirmations can boost your motivation and drive by constantly reminding you of your goals and aspirations.

- ❖ Repeating affirmations helps you stay focused on your objectives, reducing distractions and keeping you on track.

- ❖ Affirmations encourage a positive mindset, helping you to see opportunities rather than obstacles.

How Affirmations Help You Manifest Your Desires

- ❖ Affirmations help align your thoughts with your actions. When you repeatedly affirm what you want to achieve, you start to believe it's possible and take actions that support your goals.

- ❖ Affirmations create a positive mindset, which is crucial for manifestation. Positive thinking attracts positive outcomes, aligning you with the natural energy of the universe of what you want to manifest.

- ❖ Many people have deep-seated limiting beliefs that hold them back. Affirmations help challenge and replace these beliefs with more empowering ones, opening you up to new and unlimited possibilities.

- ❖ According to the Law of Attraction, what you send out attracts what is returned. Positive affirmations raise your vibrational frequency to send out and align with your true desires. Attracting similar positive energies and experiences back.

- ❖ Regular affirmations create consistency in your thoughts and emotions to shift and support your beliefs in your desires. Consistency is necessary to maintain a focused and determined approach toward achieving your goals.

Examples of Affirmations

- ❖ I am worthy of love and abundance.
- ❖ I attract positive, loving experiences in my relationship.
- ❖ I am confident and capable of having a loving and joyous relationship.
- ❖ I am happy and understanding with my partner.
- ❖ I am grateful for all the blessings in my relationship.
- ❖ My partner and I are unified and share the same vision for our relationship.

How to Use Affirmations Effectively

- ❖ Craft affirmations specific to what you want to achieve.
- ❖ Phrase affirmations in a positive manner, focusing on what you want rather than what you don't want.

- ❖ Write affirmations as if they are already happening. For example, say "I am successful" instead of "I will be successful."

- ❖ Incorporate affirmations into your daily routine. Repeat them in the morning, before bed, or anytime you need a boost.

- ❖ Say your affirmations with feeling and conviction. The more emotion you put into them, the more effective they will be.

By incorporating affirmations into your daily practice, you can reprogram your mind, align your actions with your goals, and manifest the life you desire.

It's essential to be patient and persistent. Changing your dominant frequency through years of unintentional or societal conditioning doesn't happen overnight. It requires consistent effort and mindfulness. During this process, be kind to yourself. Acknowledge that everyone has moments of negativity, and it's okay to feel down sometimes. The key is not to let those moments define your overall frequency.

Essentially, when you apply the principles of the Law of Attraction in your marriage or intimate relationship, you release the recreating force of your combined thoughts, emotions, and intentions. By consciously aligning, visualizing, and expressing gratitude, you and your partner can together shape a reality filled with love, harmony, and intimacy, expressing a deeply satisfying and flourishing partnership.

MANIFEST A JOY-FILLED RELATIONSHIP

In addition to these practices, engage in activities that bring you joy and fulfillment. Take Inspired Action by actively pursuing opportunities to align your actions with your intentions. Whether it's initiating meaningful conversations, engaging in acts of kindness, or joining in shared interests, take proactive steps to promote the relationship you desire.

Pursue hobbies and interests that make you feel good. When you are happy and content within yourself, you naturally emit a positive frequency that attracts positive experiences. Your relationship will benefit from your increased happiness and positivity.

Moreover, communicate with your partner about your intentions and efforts to harness the Law of Attraction. Encourage them to join you in this journey of positive thinking and emotional alignment. Working together towards a common goal can unify your bond and make the process more effective.

By becoming aware of your dominant frequency and consciously shifting from negative to positive, you can attract more desired and fulfilling experiences. Therefore, to emit positive frequencies, practice gratitude, visualization, positive affirmations, and joyful activities. The universe responds to the energy you put out, so choose to focus on what you want, not what you don't want. By doing so, you can create the loving, joyous, intimate, and supportive relationship you desire.

Remember, your thoughts and emotions serve as influential forces in the realm of attraction. Your thoughts are like seeds planted in the fertile soil of the universe, and your emotions act as the water that nourishes them. When you consistently focus on thoughts of love, abundance, gratitude, and empowerment, you amplify the energy of positivity and openness, thereby attracting similar vibrations from the world around you; it is the law!

Dwelling on fear, doubt, insecurity, or resentment will send out signals that repel the very experiences you desire. Negative emotions create barriers to connection and can sabotage the potential for having a meaningful relationship. By becoming aware of your thought patterns and emotional responses, you gain the power to consciously direct your energy toward creating the kind of relationship you aspire to experience.

The Law of Attraction empowers you to be a conscious co-creator of your reality within your relationship. Instead of just watching from the sidelines, wishing and hoping for the best, you actively shape the direction and essence of your relationship. By aligning your thoughts and emotions with your desires, you set off an alluring resonance that pulls those desires toward you to transform the relationship from the inside out.

Actionable Steps

- ❖ Take time to reflect on your thoughts, beliefs, and emotions regarding your relationship. Begin by gaining clarity on your own desires, values, and aspirations. Reflect on past relationships, experiences, and challenges to identify any patterns or limiting beliefs that may be hindering your ability to attract your desires in your current relationship. This helps to remove unintentional blockages.

- ❖ Clearly define what you want in your relationships with clarity and specificity. Visualize the kind of partnership you wish to attract and affirm your desires as if they have already manifested. Be extremely specific beyond surface-level answers like happiness. What does happiness look like and feel like for you? How does your partner treat you? What will you do more of together?

- ❖ Clarify your intentions for the relationship. You and your partner can write out and explain your intentions for the relationship. Articulate your shared goals and aspirations to align your energies and pave the way for intentional manifestation.

- ❖ Visualize the qualities you seek in yourself and your partner and the dynamics you aspire to experience together.

- ❖ Align your actions with your intentions by embodying the qualities you seek in your relationship. Live as if you are already in a fulfilling connection with your desire, thereby magnetizing it into your reality. Act as if whatever you want is already manifested and you are reaping the benefits right now. This helps you stay in alignment with your goals and supports your belief in their possibilities.

∞∞∞

In your journey, the Law of Attraction stands as a powerful force shaping your experiences. Through real-life examples and case studies, you witness firsthand how intentionally applying this law can transform intimate connections. These stories illustrate how individuals have harnessed the Law of Attraction to manifest significant changes in their relationships, from deepening emotional bonds to attracting compatible partners. These examples serve as tangible proof of the law's effectiveness in shaping the dynamics of love and connection.

Imagine an artist standing before a blank canvas, poised to create a masterpiece. With a clear vision of the final artwork in mind, the artist applies deliberate strokes of the brush, bringing their creation to life. Similarly, the Law of Attraction beckons you to envision your desires with clarity, filling them with positive emotions and placing trust in the magnetic forces that manifest your visions into reality.

Shared Stories

DeShon and Rita had been married for several years, but they felt a growing disconnect in their relationship over time. Determined to reignite the flame of their love, they turned to the principles of the Law of Attraction. Together, they decided to discover their individual desires and aspirations. Through practices of daily gratitude and visualization, they developed a shared vision of a deeply connected and intimate partnership.

As they immersed themselves in this process, subtle shifts began to occur within their relationship. They found themselves communicating more openly and authentically, expressing appreciation for each other's strengths and vulnerabilities. Over time, their bond deepened, and they rediscovered the joy and intimacy that had initially drawn them together. By aligning their thoughts and emotions with their shared vision, DeShon and Rita successfully manifested a renewed sense of love and connection in their marriage.

Brittani had spent years searching for a fulfilling romantic relationship but had yet to find a partner who truly resonated with her values and aspirations. Feeling disheartened, she decided to apply the principles of the Law of Attraction to her quest for love. She began by clarifying her intentions and creating a vision board that depicted her ideal partner – someone who shared her passions, supported her dreams, and embodied qualities of kindness and integrity.

With unwavering faith in the power of manifestation, Brittani began to practice self-love and empowerment. She focused on cultivating a positive mindset, releasing limiting beliefs, and radiating love and gratitude into the universe. As she remained open to new possibilities and opportunities, Brittani soon crossed paths with Lawrence, a kindred spirit she had known years before and whose values aligned perfectly with her own.

Their connection was instantaneous as if the universe had conspired to bring them together. With each passing day, their relationship blossomed, fueled by mutual respect, understanding, and affection. Through the practice of intentional manifestation, Brittani had attracted a partner who not only met but exceeded her expectations, illustrating the profound impact of the Law of Attraction in guiding us towards compatible and fulfilling relationships.

Frank and Loretta had been married for over a decade, but their relationship had grown stagnant, characterized by routine and complacency. Dissatisfied with the status quo, they decided to apply the principles of the Law of Attraction to reignite the spark in their marriage.

By consciously shifting their focus toward gratitude and appreciation for each other, they began to notice subtle yet significant improvements in their relationship dynamics. They prioritized quality time together, engaging in activities that re-ignited their passion and deepened their emotional connection.

They learned how to communicate and express their emotions without negative actions and reactions. After two weeks, they could see and feel the impact of the conscious changes on their relationship dynamics. By incorporating some of the couples' practices and techniques from this book, they transformed their marriage into a vibrant partnership, exhibiting mutual respect and affection despite their previously challenging differences.

These real-life examples serve as a testament to the potentiality of the Law of Attraction within the realm of relationships. Whether deepening emotional bonds within an existing partnership or attracting compatible partners into your life, the principles of intentional manifestation offer a powerful pathway toward love, fulfillment, and connection. As you bind the magnetic forces of your thoughts, emotions, and intentions, you ultimately unlock the limitless possibilities of co-creating the relationships you truly desire.

∞∞∞

While the Law of Attraction offers you incredible potential for transformative growth within your relationship, it's crucial to acknowledge and address common pitfalls and misconceptions. This section looks into the complexities of attraction, dispelling myths and offering guidance on navigating challenges to ensure a balanced and effective application of the law.

Despite its popularity, the Law of Attraction is often misunderstood or misinterpreted, leading to unrealistic expectations or disappointment. Common misconceptions include the belief that simply wishing for something is enough to manifest it or that the Law of Attraction guarantees a perfect, trouble-free existence. However, it's essential to recognize and steer clear of potential pitfalls and misconceptions that may impede your progress.

Successful manifestation requires more than passive wishing - it demands active participation, self-reflection, and personal growth. Additionally, while the Law of Attraction can be a powerful tool for enhancing your relationship, it does not negate the importance of effort, communication, and mutual respect in developing healthy connections.

Your external reality acts as a mirror, reflecting back the energetic vibrations you emit through your thoughts and emotions. When you find yourself surrounded by positive and harmonious experiences, it mirrors the vibrational frequencies of your positive thoughts and emotions. At the same time, challenges and discord reflect areas where your thoughts may require alignment. Be open to seeing your experiences, thoughts, and feelings from a different perspective. Therefore, be willing to adjust and align yourself where needed.

The Law of Attraction teaches you to maintain the clarity of your mental and emotional states. By doing so, you ensure that the reflections in the mirror of reality align with your true desires.

One common misconception about the Law of Attraction is the tendency to oversimplify its principles. Some individuals may perceive it as a form of wishful thinking or passive hoping, believing that merely desiring something strongly enough will inevitably bring it into their lives. However, manifestation through the Law of Attraction involves more than just thoughts; it requires deliberate alignment of thoughts, emotions, and actions. Merely wishing for a fulfilling relationship without actively working towards it is unlikely to yield significant results.

As a couple, address the importance of balance in your expectations. While intentional manifestation is powerful, unrealistic expectations can lead to disappointments, frustration, and greater disconnection. We encourage a balance between your envisioning desires and embracing your present reality.

It's essential to recognize that the Law of Attraction does not advocate for toxic positivity. Suppressing negative emotions or pretending to be happy when feeling sad, disappointed, or angry contradicts the essence of authentic manifestation. Accepting what is - as the best life has to offer, isn't living a joy-filled life. It's settling for what is because you are tired of wanting things you believe can't or won't happen. Trust in the universe to change what you can't and do your part in envisioning and believing it can.

You can embrace the full spectrum of emotions while still maintaining faith in the inherent goodness of the universe. During moments of sadness or frustration, approach these emotions with gentleness and compassion. Ask yourself, "What lessons can I derive from this experience? In what ways does this experience serve my highest good?"

Another misconception arises when individuals attribute all relationship challenges to external circumstances or the perceived deficiencies of their partner. This mindset promotes a victim mentality, where individuals feel powerless to effect change in their relationships. They may believe that if only their partner were different or if external circumstances were more favorable, their relationship would improve. However, the Law of Attraction emphasizes personal accountability and empowerment.

By recognizing your role in co-creating your relationship dynamics and taking proactive steps to shift your thoughts and behaviors, you can exert greater influence over the course of your relationship.

Therefore, we encourage you to set your intentions with clarity and openness while striving for acceptance and gratitude for the current moment. By acquiring this balance, you can enhance the journey of manifestation.

∞∞∞

The journey of intentional manifestation in your relationship inevitably involves encountering challenges and setbacks. From moments of doubt and discouragement to unexpected obstacles or rejections, maintaining faith in the process can be difficult at times.

In such moments, practice self-compassion, patience, and perseverance. Remember that setbacks are not indicative of failure but rather chances for growth and course correction. By staying aligned with your intentions, strengthening resilience, and remaining open to the possibilities that lie ahead, you can overcome challenges and continue on the path toward manifesting the relationship you desire. Remind yourself and your partner that your relationship challenges are there to help you discover what's working and what's not through awareness and opportunities.

By understanding the principles of the Law of Attraction, applying practical strategies for intentional manifestation, and overcoming common pitfalls with flexibility and determination, you can capture the power of attraction.

Also, it's vital to recognize that the Law of Attraction doesn't remove individual responsibility. As partners, you are co-creators of your relationship, and each one of you must actively contribute to the relationship's growth rather than relying solely on attraction principles or for your partner to do all the work.

You must be willing to do your part to clear energetic blockages in attraction. The role of clearing energetic blockages is paramount in facilitating attraction within your relationship. Past traumas or unresolved issues can obstruct the flow of positive energies, hindering the manifestation of desired outcomes. Techniques such as energy healing or many of the suggested practices offered in this book can aid in clearing these obstacles.

Practical Insight: Remember to incorporate these practices daily. Create mental images of your desired outcomes. Engage all your senses to make the visualization vivid and emotionally charged, amplifying the magnetic pull of your thoughts.

- ❖ Use positive affirmations to reshape your thought patterns. Affirmations serve as powerful magnets, drawing toward you the energies that resonate with the statements you declare.

- ❖ Promote a practice of gratitude to elevate your emotional state. A gratitude journal becomes a pull for positive experiences, drawing them into your life as you focus on the blessings already present.

- ❖ Welcome mindful meditation. Through mindfulness, you gain control over the chatter of the mind. This practice allows you to consciously direct your thoughts, aligning them with the vibrational frequencies of your desires. You can sit in silence, add music, or use guided meditation. Visit our website, legendaryrelationship.com, for free downloads of affirmations, gratitude practices, guided meditation, and other resources.

By acknowledging the influence of your inner world on your external experiences, you authorize yourself to consciously shape the trajectory of your relationship.

Remember, transformation takes time and requires patience, resilience, and persistence. Stay committed to your vision of a joyous and unlimited relationship, even when faced with temporary challenges and setbacks. Prioritize self-care and emotional resilience, and seek support from trusted friends, family members, life or relationship coaches, or professionals during overwhelming, challenging times. Visit our website at legendaryrelationship.com for services and referrals. Your mental state is a top priority in manifesting joyous experiences.

THE LAW OF ATTRACTION

According to the Johnnie Colemon Institute's basic principles, the fifth principle, the Law of Demonstration, reminds us: 'The Law of Mind Action: Like begets like.'

Chapter Seven
THE LAW OF COMPENSATION
Balancing Energies in Relationships

The Law of Compensation, a concept that the universe rewards you in proportion to the value you bring to others. This chapter reveals how it's not just another cosmic principle but a model for restoring balance and harmony in your interactions. By exploring the dynamics of giving and receiving, you uncover the power of generosity, gratitude, and the reciprocal nature of energy exchange. By aligning yourself with this law, you can tap into the abundant flow of the universe.

The experience of compensation as a universal law has roots in ancient philosophies and spiritual teachings and holds relevance in understanding human interactions, including relationships, on a deeper level. The notion of "what goes around comes around" reflects the essence of compensation in everyday jargon, capturing the idea that your actions return back to you in some form or fashion. This law suggests that every action has consequences, and these consequences are often proportional to the action itself. In other words, you will reap what you sow, whether in terms of effort, behavior, or intention.

Although all the laws are universally connected, you might wonder how the Laws of Compensation and Attraction differ.

THE LAW OF COMPENSATION

The Law of Attraction is about attracting what you focus on and believe in pertaining to your relationship. For example, if you focus on positive qualities and have a loving attitude, you will likely attract more love and positivity from your partner. Essentially, the energy and thoughts you put into the relationship will return to you.

On the other hand, the Law of Compensation is about getting back what you give in your relationship. For example, your partner will return the effort, kindness, and support you provide in some form or another. It emphasizes the idea that your relationship will benefit and grow in proportion to your actual, positive, intentional actions and contributions - not the ones you think you are giving.

You may disagree that what you do is not being reciprocated in the same manner you give it. Understand that you are not receiving the same actions but the thoughts and feelings behind your actions. The Law of Compensation operates on the theory that your intentions matter as much as your actions. Therefore, you may need to look through a different lens to see your intentions. Stay open during this process of rediscovery instead of looking for confirmation of your perceived actions.

This law also argues that you receive rewards or consequences that align with your actions and contributions. Don't miss that; it didn't say your partner's, but your actions and contributions. Therefore, if you are trying to be the judge and the jury for your partner's actions and consequences, you are out of alignment with the universe. Every law focuses on what you can do, not someone else. Realize that everyone will answer for their own actions, even the ones you don't understand. This law operates on the principle of balance and fairness, suggesting that there is inherent justice in the outcomes you experience based on your choices and deeds. It goes beyond cause and effect to encompass the idea of reciprocity and equilibrium in the cosmic order. Pay closer attention to what you are thinking and feeling during your time of action.

In his essay "Compensation," Ralph Waldo Emerson examines the interconnectedness of actions and consequences, emphasizing that nature maintains a balance and that individuals cannot escape the consequences of their choices.

Simply put, in attraction, you get what you focus on, and in compensation, you get what you give. So, if you think the universe is unfair, check your intentions, not necessarily your actions. Action may speak louder than words, but not louder than intentions.

∞∞∞

Paramount to the Law of Compensation in relationships is reciprocity - the give-and-take that forms the foundation of healthy interactions. Mutual respect, trust, and empathy are vital ingredients that sustain meaningful relationships and contribute to their growth and stability.

This law highlights the reciprocal nature of give and receive within your relationship. It implies that the universe responds to your thoughts, feelings, and actions by providing compensation in kind. Understanding this law becomes critical for ensuring a balanced and harmonious exchange.

Research on the impact of generosity and selflessness on well-being underscores the positive outcomes associated with acts of kindness and consideration within partnerships.

THE LAW OF COMPENSATION

Examining compensation principles gives us a deeper understanding of how our contributions shape our relational landscape.

Each partner brings their unique strengths, values, and contributions. The Law of Compensation encourages us to recognize and value these contributions to gain appreciation and fairness. This recognition also extends to acknowledging responsibilities and commitments in fulfilling your role and how it contributes to the relationship's overall well-being.

Mindful giving becomes a focal point, encouraging you to offer support, affection, and understanding with intention and awareness. Techniques such as exploring love languages and empathy-building exercises enhance communication and create positive compensatory dynamics.

Aligning and upholding your personal values and ethical standards is integral in applying the Law of Compensation to your relationship. When you align your actions and behaviors with values such as honesty, integrity, empathy, and compassion, you create a positive environment conducive to a healthy connection. Nevertheless, unintentionally engaging in actions contradicting these values leads to conflicts and challenges.

By embracing a mindset of abundance and reciprocity, couples have fostered environments where positive actions are met with positive responses, creating a cycle of mutual benefit.

Shared story

Antón and Alexis entered their relationship carrying emotional baggage from past traumas and failed relationships. The Law of Compensation guided them in overcoming these challenges and being open to emotional healing and understanding.

Antón and Alexis acknowledged the emotional wounds and triggers that affected their interactions and intimacy. They realized that unresolved issues from past relationships, upbringing, and unproven beliefs could hinder their relationship's growth and connection.

Instead of blaming each other for their emotional struggles, Antón and Alexis took individual responsibility for their healing journey. They individually sought personal development coaching and participated in couples' coaching to address communication barriers, emotional vulnerabilities, and how to speak each other's love language. They purchased their first-ever relationship course to help them learn, apply, and practice how to take their relationship from being on the brink of ruin to finding new joy and intimacy that they thought was lost and unattainable. Visit legendaryrelationship.com/coaching for more information and services.

The couple shifted their perspectives and aligned their actions with healing processes, such as practicing active listening, expressing emotions authentically, speaking and expressing love to their partner, and practicing forgiveness and empathy. They also engaged in activities promoting self-care and emotional well-being, such as shared meditation, exercising, and journaling.

THE LAW OF COMPENSATION

By embracing vulnerability, empathy, love languages, and a commitment to personal and relational healing and learning, Antón and Alexis experienced profound shifts in their relationship. They developed deeper empathy for each other's past experiences, learned to communicate more effectively about sensitive topics, and established a stronger emotional bond grounded in trust and acceptance. Instead of looking at their past as reasons why they couldn't make the relationship work, they realized that it enriched their separate and shared journey. Through coaching and using proven tools and techniques given in this book, they were able to learn from their past and move into a brighter future together. Recognizing the law's intrinsic value cultivates positive actions, reactions, and reciprocity.

∞∞∞

To use the law of compensation to create a happy and healthy relationship, you must understand and effectively manage compensation dynamics. This section details some of the difficulties of compensation dynamics and helps you identify key areas where compensation plays a crucial role and impacts relationship aspects.

Emotional support and empathy form the basis of a healthy relationship. You and your partners can compensate for each other's emotional needs by actively listening, empathizing, and offering comfort throughout your relationship. This involves you collectively creating a safe space for open communication where you and your partner can share and feel heard and valued, promoting a sense of security.

Another area where compensation dynamics come into play is managing and contributing to household responsibilities. Distributing responsibilities based on capabilities and availability promotes fairness, reduces stress, and avoids one-sided obligations. When you routinely express gratitude and appreciation for each other's contributions to managing household tasks, this reinforces your mutual respect and acknowledgment of shared responsibilities. Equitably sharing chores and tasks ensures that neither partner feels overburdened and develops a sense of teamwork and cooperation.

The financial aspects of a relationship require careful consideration and mutual understanding. This involves you and your partner contributing to financial discussions, setting joint financial goals, and making decisions to improve the overall relationship regardless of who feels better equipped. Involving both partners in financial discussions and decision-making promotes transparency and shared accountability. Collaborative budgeting, shared financial responsibilities, and transparent communication are crucial components of compensation dynamics. It does not matter if your finances are in one bank account or two. Your shared responsibilities are just that, shared. Both partners must feel knowledgeable and secure in ensuring all financial obligations are met. Sharing financial burdens, being transparent about income, expenses, and savings, and making joint decisions contribute to financial stability and trust within your relationship, extending beyond the financial scope and reducing unnecessary conflicts.

Shared story

Sahed and Morgan have been married for five years and recently faced significant financial challenges due to unexpected medical expenses and job instability. Applying the Law of Compensation, they approached the situation with mutual support and collaboration.

Sahed and Morgan acknowledged the financial strain and its impact on their daily lives. They recognized that their previous financial decisions, such as overspending and lack of emergency savings, contributed to their current challenges.

Sahed and Morgan appreciated each other's efforts despite the challenges. Sahed took on extra freelance work to supplement their income, while Morgan diligently managed the household budget, finding ways to cut unnecessary expenses.

The couple aligned their financial decisions with their shared values of responsibility and long-term planning. They prioritized essential expenses, communicated openly about financial concerns, and sought guidance from financial advisors to create a sustainable budget and savings plan.

Through their concerted efforts and adherence to the principles of the Law of Compensation, Sahed and Morgan not only overcame their immediate financial hurdles but also strengthened their communication, trust, and shared commitment to financial stability.

The significant impact of fair and balanced compensation dynamics contributes to your building trust, mutual respect, and a sense of partnership. When you and your partner feel valued and appreciated for your contributions, it strengthens the basic foundation of your relationship.

Realize that compensation dynamics play a fundamental role in managing conflicts and resolving disagreements constructively. Fairness in exchanges and mutual understanding reduces the likelihood of resentment and promotes effective communication during challenging times.

Mutual compensation also promotes a sense of partnership and teamwork within your relationship. When you collaborate, support each other, and work towards common goals, you create a shared sense of accomplishment, fulfillment, and enhancement in your relationship satisfaction.

Identifying these compensation dynamics enables you to construct a supportive and balanced relationship where both partners feel acknowledged and emotionally invested. It lays the groundwork for effective communication, conflict resolution, and mutual growth, leading to a lasting and successful partnership.

∞∞∞

This section explores practical strategies for effectively applying compensation principles, emphasizing the importance of open communication, negotiation, and empathy.

You and your partner should feel comfortable discussing your expectations, needs, and concerns openly, without fear of judgment or misunderstanding. Clear communication helps align your expectations and prevents misunderstandings, so it's important to express your needs, desires, and boundaries openly while actively listening to each other's perspectives. When conflicts arise, address them promptly and constructively using "I" statements, active listening techniques, and negotiate to find mutually acceptable solutions.

THE LAW OF COMPENSATION

Successful relationships require a willingness to negotiate and sometimes agree to disagree. As you negotiate, remember this involves finding common ground and settlements that satisfy both partners. This may include brainstorming options, considering each other's perspectives, and being flexible in finding solutions. Your relationship has and will evolve over time. Therefore, it's essential for you to be able to adapt to changing circumstances. Flexibility and willingness to adjust plans or expectations help maintain harmony and resilience. Both you and your partner should be open to finding mutually beneficial solutions that honor each other's needs and preferences while respecting each other's opinions and boundaries.

Empathy involves imagining oneself in the other person's position and understanding their emotions and motivations. During difficult situations, offer empathy, validation, and support to strengthen your bond and reinforce or reestablish a sense of partnership. It helps if you strive to understand each other's feelings, perspectives, and experiences, even during challenging times.

In effectively applying the Law of Compensation, partners prioritize each other's career aspirations while effectively managing family responsibilities. This may involve flexible work arrangements, shared childcare responsibilities, and mutual support in pursuing professional goals. Partners support each other's career growth while ensuring adequate time and attention to family needs, creating a balanced and fulfilling life.

Often, when one partner feels neglected or carries the burden of all or most of the relationship's responsibilities by themselves, they will retreat by physically and emotionally pulling away from their partner. This act indicates that you seek love, respect, and appreciation, not isolation.

First, consider implementing self-development techniques and learning tools for effective communication. After feeling comfortable with a new awareness, skills, and a willingness to overcome your relationship challenges, begin to create a safe space for sharing where you can be open and honest about your feelings and your desire to reconnect and start healing.

Shared story

Troy and LaCheryl, both career-driven individuals, struggled to balance their demanding jobs with family responsibilities and quality time together. The Law of Compensation guided them to find a harmonious equilibrium and prioritize their relationship amidst busy schedules.

Troy and LaCheryl acknowledged the imbalances in their time allocation and emotional energy due to work pressures. They realized that neglecting their relationship could lead to resentment and strain.

Despite their career aspirations, Troy and LaCheryl shared the goal of maintaining a solid and connected relationship. They discussed their priorities and identified areas where they could make adjustments to prioritize quality time together.

Alignment with Time Management - The couple implemented strategies to maximize the quality of their time together, such as setting aside dedicated date nights, creating a shared calendar for family activities, and practicing active listening during conversations.

THE LAW OF COMPENSATION

By proactively addressing work-life balance challenges and aligning their actions with their shared values, Troy and LaCheryl experienced a renewed sense of closeness and fulfillment in their relationship. They found that investing time and effort in nurturing their bond strengthened their resilience and happiness individually and as a couple.

Regular expressions of love, appreciation, and emotional support contribute to gaining a deep and meaningful connection with your partner. Taking time for shared activities, intimate conversations, and moments of affection strengthens the emotional bond and reinforces the Law of Compensation in emotional exchanges. Remember to start small with things you both enjoy, then incorporate partner-specific interests where the experience is shared by learning and supporting one another.

By implementing these strategies, you learn to handle challenges effectively, enhance mutual understanding and partnership, and build a resilient and satisfying relationship based on fairness, communication, and empathy. The Law of Compensation is a roadmap for a successful partnership where you and your partner can feel valued, heard, and supported, leading to long-term relationship satisfaction.

"It's not how much we give but how much love we put into giving." - Mother Teresa.

Mother Teresa's wisdom captures the essence of the Law of Compensation. It prompts you to consider the quality of your contributions within your relationship, emphasizing that the energy you invest determines the nature of the compensation you receive. By infusing your actions with love and intention, you pave the way for a cycle of positive reciprocity.

Despite its potential for promoting fairness and balance, the Law of Compensation in relationships can face challenges and pitfalls that require careful navigation. To overcome these obstacles, we offer strategies for common challenges you may face in practicing compensation principles.

One of the most prevalent challenges in relationships is the risk of giving-and-taking imbalance. When one partner consistently invests more effort, time, or emotional energy, giving the illusion of unequal contributions or unmet expectations without receiving equitable reciprocity, it can lead to feelings of resentment and dissatisfaction.

- ❖ Encourage open dialogue about perceived imbalances.

- ❖ Establish clear expectations.

- ❖ Work towards a fair distribution of responsibilities and efforts.

Implementing regular check-ins to assess the balance of contributions can also help prevent resentment from building up. Communication is vitally important in this area. Your assumption that your partner knows your feelings and why is an unspoken expectation. It isn't fair to them or to you. Manifesting your desires requires starting from where you are working on issues and learning how to overcome them together.

THE LAW OF COMPENSATION

Variations in expectations, values, and communication styles between partners can create friction. Misaligned expectations regarding roles, responsibilities, or levels of support can lead to misunderstandings and conflicts in compensating efforts and understanding each other's needs.

- ❖ Create shared, effective communication to understand each other's expectations and values.

- ❖ Practice listening strategies, shift your perspective to view things differently, and give full cooperation to find common ground and respect individual differences.

- ❖ If significant discrepancies persist, seek professional guidance through couples' coaching or relationship courses to gain new skills, elevate your awareness, and move beyond reoccurring challenges. Visit legendaryrelationship.com/coaching.

Another necessary factor to remember is that you cannot correct a problem at the level it was created. You need to gain the skill set to work through your challenges. Therefore, the tools and techniques in this book are a good starting point. However, depending on each situation and relationship, more outside help may be required. Therefore, feel free to book a discovery call with us to help you on your journey at legendaryrelationship.com/discover.

External factors such as societal norms, cultural expectations, financial stressors, or family dynamics can impact relationship compensation dynamics. These external pressures may introduce additional challenges and strain on your partnership.

- ❖ Openly recognize and discuss external pressures affecting your relationship.

- ❖ Establish boundaries and priorities together and work collaboratively to resolve external challenges as a team.

- ❖ Seek support from trusted friends, family members, or relationship coaches who can provide valuable insights and guidance.

Relationships evolve, and it's important to reassess and adjust your expectations periodically. Regular check-ins and discussions about goals, needs, and roles help maintain alignment and prevent miscommunications or resentments from escalating when adapting to changing circumstances and learning to avoid conflict.

Building resilience and mutual support strengthens your relationship's foundation. To resolve challenges collaboratively, you can work on building trust, practicing forgiveness, and promoting a sense of teamwork. Developing a supportive and resilient partnership through shared experiences, trust-building activities, and mutual understanding strengthens your relationship's ability to overcome challenges. You can overcome obstacles when practicing the Law of Compensation by proactively addressing common challenges, adapting to changing circumstances, and prioritizing mutual understanding and support.

THE LAW OF COMPENSATION

This chapter's stories illustrate how the Law of Compensation can be applied in diverse marriage and intimate relationship scenarios. Whether facing financial hardships, emotional struggles, or balancing competing priorities, the principles of fairness, reciprocity, and conscious decision-making guided these couples toward understanding, growth, and harmony in their relationships. By learning from these examples and integrating the principles of the Law of Compensation in your relationship, you can handle your relationship challenges with a shared commitment to mutual well-being.

According to Charles Fillmore in *The Revealing Word* (1959, reprinted 2014, Martino Publishing), "The law of compensation is universal and not subject to personal demands" (p. 39).

Chapter Eight
THE LAW OF PERPETUAL TRANSMUTATION OF ENERGY
The Impact of Positive and Negative Energy Flow

In the vastness of the universe, where energy reigns supreme, you will find the Law of Perpetual Transmutation of Energy. Its essence is grounded in a simple yet profound truth that everything in the universe is in a constant state of flow, perpetually changing from one form to another. This law, not just a cosmic force but a fundamental principle, yields the transformative power of energy and its innate ability to shape your relationship. By understanding and using this law, you become part of that flow connected to the energy that shapes the universe and your relationship, allowing you to form your reality.

This concept suggests that energy is constantly in motion, transforming from one form to another. Therefore, the energy within your relationship is always changing form, never created or destroyed. This means that the energy within your relationship is constantly transmuting and evolving. Your positive or negative thoughts and actions can transform this energy, impacting your experiences and reality. Consciously directing and elevating your energy allows you to transcend limitations and channel the creative power within, intentionally shaping the thoughts and emotions you have for a healthier relationship.

THE LAW OF PERPETUAL TRANSMUTATION OF ENERGY

Actively managing this energy flow is crucial for manifesting love, connection, and growth.

∞∞∞∞

This law, established in the active nature of energetic currents, explains that energy is always in a state of flow and transformation. Every interaction, whether conscious or subconscious, verbal or nonverbal, generates energy. This energy can be positive, improving love, understanding, and growth, or negative, fueling conflicts, misunderstandings, and resentment. Recognizing and harnessing this energy flow is necessary for those seeking unconditional love and longevity.

The impact of positive or negative energy flow on your relationship cannot be overstated. Positive energy increases intimacy, trust, and support between you and your partner, creating an environment where both of you can thrive and feel satisfied. It fortifies your bond, deepens emotional connections, and enhances your overall well-being, providing a sense of reassurance and security. On the flip side, negative energy can be detrimental, leading to distrust, conflict, and emotional distance. It can manifest as hidden conflicts and create unnecessary trials and tribulations.

Negative energy may stem from unresolved conflicts, unmet needs, or past traumas. If left unaddressed, it can destroy your relationship, breeding resentment and disconnection. By consciously shifting negative energy, you can convert that energy into positive outcomes, encouraging you to take control of your relationship's dynamics.

Realizing that energy manifests in various vibrational frequencies is significant to how these frequencies shape your experiences and circumstances. This law urges you to participate actively in the continuous process of transmutation, elevating your lower frequencies to higher, more harmonious ones. Following this law becomes critical in unlocking the transformative potential inherent in the shared energy between you and your partner.

As you and your partner evolve and adapt, you contribute to the energy of your relationship. This law shows how supporting each other's growth fits the idea that energy constantly evolves. Therefore, instead of resisting change, welcome it into your relationship with loving intentions and positive vibes with hope and optimism for a happy and loving future.

∞∞∞

This section offers techniques for successfully transforming negative energy within the Law of Perpetual Transmutation of Energy. These techniques include mindfulness, cognitive restructuring, joint activities, gratitude practices, and harnessing the energy flow within and around you to elevate your mental and physical activity. There are numerous others; feel free to explore and use what fits your personality and relationship.

One powerful technique for transforming negative energy is mindfulness. You can interrupt the pattern and choose a different response by becoming aware of the thoughts, emotions, and behaviors contributing to negative energy. Challenges and change are inevitable; embrace them. They are opportunities for elevated awareness in unhealthy and undeveloped areas in your relationship. Strategies for emotional regulation and mindfulness provide you with practices to stay in control during emotional fluctuations.

THE LAW OF PERPETUAL TRANSMUTATION OF ENERGY

Remember, you hold the power to consciously steer the flow of energy in your life. Just as a river can be controlled and redirected through intentional channels, your thoughts, emotions, and actions can serve as conduits for energy flow. By actively choosing thoughts and feelings aligned with higher vibrational frequencies - such as love, gratitude, and joy - you enhance the quality of your relationship by redirecting your energy.

Reframing is another transformative strategy that invites you to view challenges as progression and learning. Cognitive restructuring, a powerful cognitive-behavioral therapy technique, allows you to reframe negative thought patterns and support a positive mindset. Instead of dwelling on negativity or assigning blame, you can shift your perspective and uncover hidden solutions and resources within yourself and your relationship. This process of reframing allows you to change the narrative, transforming the outcome from a negative experience to one that is neutral or finding the silver lining.

Joint activities are not just about spending time together; they are powerful tools for transforming negative energy into positive experiences. Whether it's taking a walk, cooking together, or practicing a hobby, these moments of togetherness can reignite feelings of love and appreciation. They create a space for joy and connection, dissipating negative energy and opening up the channels for more positive experiences to occur.

Intentionally incorporating a daily gratitude practice transforms and builds an appreciation for the positive aspects of life. Whether through a gratitude journal, gratitude jar, gratitude letter, or verbal expressions, acknowledging blessings, ones often overlooked and those earth-shattering, amplifies the transmutation of energy toward positivity. Integrating positive affirmations into your daily routine reinforces a constructive mindset. These intentional statements act as stimuli for transmuting lower vibrational energies, optimism, and empowerment. Engaging in creative endeavors also channels and transforms negative energy toward higher frequencies. Through art, music, writing, and other forms of expression, you facilitate the flow of positivity, enriching your inner being and outer world.

Harness and transform the energy within and around you to elevate your mental and physical activity. This energy, which can also be described as vitality or enthusiasm, impacts your overall liveliness and spirit. To facilitate this transformation, be mindful of the content you consume, choosing things that resonate with positive energy. Transmuting energy sometimes requires altering the constants in your life - whether it's the music you listen to, the media you engage with, the friendships you maintain, or the experiences you immerse yourself in. Prioritize and select interactions that contribute to your ongoing positivity. Understand that it's perfectly acceptable to love people, situations, or things from a distance until you can maintain a higher state of mind and awareness. Embrace the necessity of change, knowing that if nothing changes, nothing changes. By doing so, you can effectively transmute energy to support a more vibrant and fulfilling life.

∞∞∞∞

Communication is a foundational stone in transmuting energy within your relationship. It serves as the primary tool through which thoughts, emotions, and intentions are expressed and received. Effective communication adopts understanding, supports empathy, and strengthens the emotional connection between you and your partner. However, poor communication can breed misunderstanding, bitterness, and discord, perpetuating negative energy within your relationship. A healthy relationship is acquired through both partners learning to express their needs and concerns through effective communication channels.

Communication skills are prevalent as a means of transmuting energy within your relationship. Techniques that promote nonviolent communication and active listening increase mutual understanding, providing a platform for transforming discordant energies into opportunities for connection and development.

Communication is the bridge through which energy flows between you and your partner. By understanding the vibrational nature of words and expressions, you enhance your communication to positively influence the transmutation of energy within your relationship.

Communication serves as your primary vehicle for energy transmutation, where you can genuinely express your thoughts, feelings, and needs. This openness unifies understanding and empathy between you both. By practicing active listening without judgment, interruptions, or defensiveness, you learn to validate your partner's experiences and perspectives, reinforcing your sense of connection and mutual respect. Your differences in perspective are what make you unique. Instead of trying to change each other, focus on understanding how your partner thinks and feels.

Nevertheless, effective communication equips you and your partner to address conflicts constructively. Instead of blaming or criticizing, you can engage in collaborative problem-solving, seeking solutions that honor both partner's needs and values for transparency. This transparency enables you to express your emotions openly and authentically. By rationally sharing your feelings, you create an atmosphere of emotional intelligence and vulnerability. Through active listening and empathetic responses, you enhance mutual support and acceptance. Communicating with kindness, compassion, and humility, you transform negative energy into positive outcomes. Effective communication highlights the practical value of communication in maintaining a healthy relationship.

Conflict is a predictable aspect of any relationship, especially intimate ones. However, how you communicate during times of conflict determines whether the energy is transmuted constructively or escalates into further discord. Healthy communication strategies like active listening, non-defensive responding, and seeking cooperation facilitate the resolution of conflicts with minimal negative impact on the relationship. Addressing conflicts immediately and respectfully can convert tension and bitterness into insight and intimacy.

Communication also plays a crucial role in setting intentions and creating a shared vision for your relationship. When you learn to engage in nonjudgmental dialogue about your goals, values, and aspirations, you align your energies toward common objectives. This shared sense of purpose further enhances cohesion and unity within your relationship, enabling you to overcome obstacles together. Regularly reaffirming your commitment to each other and clearly communicating your intentions create a positive energy that sustains your relationship through life's challenges. Simple, yet meaningful conversations and expressing appreciation for each other strengthen the emotional bond you share. Through words of affirmation, acts of kindness, and expressions of love, you transform ordinary moments into chances for intense connection and joy. By prioritizing communication, you create trust and closeness that can sustain your relationship.

In essence, communication serves as a powerful mechanism for energy transmutation. Engaging in positive dialogue, resolving conflicts constructively, setting intentions, and improving connection, you learn to channel the transformative power of communication to maintain a relationship grounded in love, understanding, and mutual respect.

∞∞∞

At the depth of this law lies the recognition that your thoughts and emotions carry considerable influence over the energy surrounding your relationship. Therefore, you can consciously transmute negative thoughts and feelings into positive ones by creating an atmosphere of love, understanding, and compassion by how you communicate. Here are some communication practices that can facilitate positive energy transmutation.

Practices

- ❖ Listening to your partner without interruption by giving your full attention, keeping eye contact, and reflecting back on what you've heard to ensure your comprehension. This demonstrates respect for your partner's perspective, a willingness to resolve conflicts, and restore your emotional connection.

❖ Empathizing with your partner's feelings and experiences is mandatory for emotional connection. It takes maturity to listen and validate your partner's emotions by acknowledging their validity. Expressing empathy helps transmute negative emotions into positive energy for better outcomes and future experiences.

❖ Expressing your own thoughts, feelings, and needs by being clear and assertive. Avoid passive-aggressive communication or resorting to blame and criticism. Use "I" statements to express your feelings and avoid the need to repeat issues or defend your actions. Practice constructive conflict resolution skills and aim for win-win solutions. Avoid escalating conflicts by using respectful language and taking breaks when emotions run high - approach conflicts with empathy and a willingness to find resolutions that encourage productive solution-based communication.

❖ Scheduling regular check-ins to discuss the state of your relationship and address any concerns or challenges. Use check-ins to express positive aspects of your relationship, such as appreciation for each other and shared goals, to reinforce your commitment to the relationship. Regular communication facilitates the ongoing transmutation of energy toward positivity and progression.

THE LAW OF PERPETUAL TRANSMUTATION OF ENERGY

Therefore, don't be fooled. What you say, how you say it, and the energy behind what you say matters.

∞∞∞

The Law of Perpetual Transmutation of Energy, a concept particularly relevant to relationships, teaches you that energy constantly shifts and changes no matter what. Instead of resisting change, expect it, learn from it, and transform it. Embrace challenges for personal and relational resilience and perseverance, knowing that each experience brings with it untapped potential.

Resilience and perseverance in your relationship involve controlling the transformative power of positive focus, gratitude, and love. Through intentional practices grounded in the Law of Perpetual Transmutation of Energy, relationships can thrive amidst adversity, demonstrating grit and enduring connection.

Resilience is the strength to overcome setbacks, adapt to change, and prosper in challenging situations. Within your relationship, resilience is essential for weathering the expected storms that arise along the way. Building resilience requires self-awareness, self-regulation, and coping skills that enable you to handle difficult emotions and situations gracefully and with courage. Refocus your attention not on the issue but on the desired outcome.

Perseverance plays a vital role in developing resilience within your relationship. Psychological research highlights the significance of resilience in overcoming adversity and productively adapting to life's challenges. By incorporating resilience-building practices, you can work through difficulties with a sense of perseverance and grit.

One way to develop resilience is through self-care practices that nourish the mind, body, and spirit. Engaging in relaxation activities like journaling, exercising, biking, or swimming can replenish depleted energy stores and enhance emotional well-being.

Taking care of yourself is also essential for building resilience in your relationship. Prioritize self-care practices that nourish your physical, emotional, and spiritual well-being. Make time for activities that bring you joy, relaxation, and fulfillment: practice mindfulness, meditation, and stress-reduction techniques to cultivate inner peace and resilience. By prioritizing your well-being, you can show up as your best self, contributing to the overall resilience of your relationship. Your well-being is a crucial component of your relationship's strength.

Positive thinking is a powerful for building resilience. You can turn negative energy into positive outcomes by consciously directing your focus toward positive aspects of your life, relationship, and partner. Adopting a positive mindset enhances your resilience and allows you to shift your perspective on how you view challenges.

Your partner's support is one of the greatest sources of resilience in relationships. Lean on each other during difficult times, offering emotional support, encouragement, and reassurance. Share your burdens and vulnerabilities openly, knowing you are stronger together than apart. By facing challenges as a united front, you can transmute adversity into anything you want it to be.

THE LAW OF PERPETUAL TRANSMUTATION OF ENERGY

By embracing challenges and change, ensuring a positive mindset, communicating, leaning on each other for support, and including self-care and well-being, you can overcome difficulties with grace and grit.

∞∞∞

The Law of Perpetual Transmutation of Energy is significant in understanding the dynamics of relationships, particularly the importance of adopting a growth mindset. Adopting a growth mindset is essential for demonstrating resilience, overcoming challenges, and embodying a thriving partnership.

As psychologist Carol Dweck coined it, a growth mindset is the belief that intelligence, abilities, and relationships can be developed through effort, learning, and perseverance. It entails recognizing that challenges and setbacks are special occasions for learning and developing skills rather than insurmountable obstacles. Adopting this mindset gives you a sense of optimism, adaptability, and empowerment within your relationship.

"In the middle of difficulty lies opportunity." - Albert Einstein

Einstein's perception is invaluable in how you should perceive your relationship challenges. It urges you to perceive difficulties as steppingstones for personal and relational growth to unlock the potential inherent in challenges, propelling your connections to newfound heights.

A growth mindset embodies the same essence and encourages you to view challenges within your relationship as steppingstones for transformation. Instead of being discouraged by obstacles, a growth mindset approaches them with curiosity and resilience, knowing there are underdeveloped areas in your life and relationship.

With a growth mindset, feedback and criticism are seen as valuable lessons for learning and improvement rather than personal attacks. Just as negative energy can be transmuted to positive energy, constructive feedback can be transmuted into possibilities for personal and relational enhancement. You welcome constructive input from each other with sincerity and humility, using it as awareness for self-reflection and positive change.

A growth mindset inspires you to view conflict as an experience for reconciliation and evolution rather than avoidance or escalation. Couples with a growth mindset develop practical communication skills and seek mutually beneficial solutions. Through intentional practices based on the principles of energy transmutation, you can manifest a relationship that changes and flourishes over time.

∞∞∞∞

Harmonizing with the Law of Perpetual Transmutation of Energy involves aligning your consciousness with universal principles. By consciously choosing thoughts and emotions resonating with love and abundance, you sync with the natural flow of the universe. This alignment initiates a continuous process of transmutation, wherein the energy you emit attracts corresponding energies, perpetually elevating your vibrational frequency.

Love, the most potent energy in the universe, becomes your focal point in applying the Law of Perpetual Transmutation of Energy. You can improve and amplify the power of

THE LAW OF PERPETUAL TRANSMUTATION OF ENERGY

love, creating a magnetic field that strengthens your bond by tapping into the energic field of universal love.

Abundance, in its countless forms, naturally manifests within your relationship through the law. When you consciously align with the energy of abundance, you invite a steady flow of prosperity into your relationship. Just like an unobstructed river nourishes the land it touches; the power of abundance enriches every facet of your partnership when allowed to flow freely through positive focus and intentional actions.

Through understanding, embracing, and actively applying this law, you can unlock the transformative power within your relationship, crafting your unique bond of perpetual love and growth.

> With every disappointment, heartbreak, or failure, there exists an equal "usually greater" positive benefit.
>
> Napoleon Hill, regarding the Law of Transmutation

Chapter Nine
THE LAW OF RELATIVITY
Putting Challenges into
Perspective Within Relationships

The Law of Relativity is a reflective principle in relationships that urges you to view challenges within the broader context of life. This law equips you with the discernment to steer your relationship through inevitable difficulties. It teaches that the nature of your challenges is not absolute but rather dependent on your perspectives and interpretations. Therefore, understanding and mastering the power of relativity can be a game-changer in transforming your relationship, making you more knowledgeable and prepared.

As you progress through the laws, maintaining an open mind, it's crucial to be aware of your own biases. Understanding the psychological dynamics of cognitive distortions and how they influence your perception of your relationship satisfaction can lead to a higher level of self-awareness. Self-awareness is the key that sparks transformation, enlightening and guiding you from a vulnerable crawling caterpillar to a wise soaring butterfly. It enables you to shift your perspective to a higher state of consciousness, seeing beyond appearances to a level of understanding of the deeper dynamics of your thoughts, feelings, and behaviors. Perception plays a crucial role in determining your biases' significance and impact.

∞∞∞

The law is a concept with practical implications in relationships stating that everything is relative and gains meaning through your comparison. This means that all your experiences are relative to your perception, much like different shades of color on a spectrum where each hue has its value compared to others. The meaning of your experiences depends on where they fall within your perception's spectrum. Therefore, you see your relationship challenges not in isolation but from the larger perspective of your life.

For example, financial struggles may be a source of stress for one couple. In contrast, another couple may view them as an opportunity for growth and collaboration. Similarly, conflicts over household responsibilities may arise from differing expectations and experiences. What one couple perceives as a minor disagreement may be perceived as a major conflict by another. This highlights the relativity of challenges and stresses the importance of recognizing and respecting each other's perspectives despite how far apart on the spectrum they may seem.

In your relationship, perception is the window through which you interpret and respond to your shared reality. Your previous experiences, faith, and state of consciousness, along with other factors, also shape your perception. What you may perceive as an act of love or support may be viewed differently by your partner, pointing out the subjective nature of your relational experiences.

The law also suggests that everything is neutral; labels such as good or bad, rich or poor, or enough or not enough merely reflect one's personal experiences and relationships. For example, the perception of earning $30 an hour varies greatly depending on one's past income and lifestyle. Similarly, the size of an 1,800-square-foot house may be perceived as either large or small depending on someone's past living arrangements.

Perception not only influences how you interpret your partner's actions but also affects your attitudes, beliefs, and expectations within your relationship. For example, a partner who perceives themselves as undervalued or unappreciated may interpret neutral gestures from their partner as evidence of neglect or indifference. However, a partner with a positive perception of their relationship may view the same gestures as expressions of love and care.

The relativity of challenges extends beyond the individual level to encompass cultural, societal, and familial influences. Each partner brings their own set of values, beliefs, expectations, and experiences to the relationship. Cultural norms, gender roles, and societal expectations can shape how you perceive your role and responsibilities. For example, traditional gender norms may influence the perceptions of household duties, childcare responsibilities, and decision-making authority, which, in turn, have a direct effect on your relationship.

Often, limiting beliefs arise from your narrow perspective within your spectrum of relativity. The Law of Relativity, however, allows you to recognize and rise above those constraints by expanding your viewpoints. Just as a door opens to reveal the vastness behind it, broadening your perspective unlocks doors to new views and possibilities. Imagine and see your relationship not as it currently is, but with boundless possibilities as you challenge your limiting beliefs around your challenges. This perspective gives you the power to shape your relationship's narrative regardless of its challenges.

∞∞∞

Relationships are active entities characterized by constant fluctuations and changes. We all enter relationships with preconceived notions and expectations based on our past experiences, beliefs, cultural and societal influences, and fallacies from Disney movies. These perceptions shape how you view your partner's behavior, communicate your needs, and resolve conflicts. For instance, a couple from different cultural backgrounds may face challenges related to communication styles, family dynamics, and social expectations. This doesn't mean their relationship is doomed. It only suggests that they must understand these differences and learn how to overcome them by improving their relationship skills.

Your perception interprets, interacts with, and makes sense of your relational experiences. Even if you and your partner face the same situation, your perceptions might differ because of your individual backgrounds, beliefs, emotional states, and family influence. What may seem like an impossible challenge to you might be perceived as a minor inconvenience by your partner or vice-versa.

For instance, a disagreement over household chores might be a significant issue for you, while your partner might not see it as a big deal. Let's say your partner grew up in a household where emotions were suppressed and struggles to express vulnerability or intimacy, impacting your interactions with one another. Without understanding your partner's struggles, you may interpret their behavior as not caring, unloving, and insensitive.

Perception is 90% influenced by your past in interpreting and responding to the world around you. They fool you into believing that your notions, expectations, and beliefs are right, even though you have never challenged their validity. Therefore, recognizing the relativity of your situations and challenges is essential for maintaining mindfulness and awareness of your personal biases. By consciously shifting your perspective, you can begin to develop gratitude and appreciation in all situations. You can avoid comparing your relationship to others or holding unrealistic expectations of yourself and your partner. This practice provides contentment and enriches every area of your life experiences. To perceive differently, you must actively challenge your existing beliefs and assumptions. This involves being open to new experiences and continuously learning. And maybe even concluding that you may be wrong - sometimes!

In other words, instead of dismissing or minimizing each other's behaviors or concerns, strive to understand and even empathize with each other's perspectives. This recognition shows that you value your experiences and your partner's, no matter how different. You can approach each situation with a different mindset to overcome challenges constructively.

Improving your awareness of your own perceptions and biases allows you to approach conflicts and challenges with greater clarity and understanding. Reframing your perceptions and challenging ingrained beliefs can create space for growth, healing, and transformation within your relationship. This lays the groundwork for open communication, finding balance, and connecting in areas you may have previously struggled. Ultimately, embracing the relativity of perception allows you to conquer the complexities of love, trust, and intimacy and opens the door to a future filled with grace, resilience, and mutual respect. This understanding offers a hopeful and optimistic outlook for your relationship's potential.

∞∞∞

Realizing that everything is relative and the meaning you assign to events and experiences is contingent upon your perspective can be truly beneficial in your relationship, particularly when resolving conflicts. Central to this process is the power of perspective-taking, a tool that can empower you to consider another's viewpoint empathetically.

Addressing and working together to resolve conflicts can greatly impact the health and longevity of your union and emotional connection. By intentionally engaging in a relative perspective and incorporating perspective-taking exercises, you can transcend your individual viewpoint and gain a higher awareness of the underlying motivations and needs driving your relational conflicts. This empathic understanding paves the way for constructive dialogue, cooperation, and collaborative problem-solving, strengthening the relational bond in the process.

It allows you to step outside of your own worldview and empathize with your partner's point of view. Instead of focusing solely on your own needs and desires, you can energetically listen and support your partner's feelings and experiences. This promotes mutual respect and compassion in collectively finding solutions. The more you practice perspective-taking, the more impactful the benefits are on your relationship dynamically.

In times of conflict and frustration, let us remember that this law supports The St. Francis Prayer - *Make Me an Instrument of Your Peace*.

Lord, make me an instrument of your peace,

Where there is hatred, let me sow love;

Where there is injury, pardon;

Where there is doubt, faith;

Where there is despair, hope;

Where there is darkness, light;

Where there is sadness, joy;

O Divine Master,

Grant that I may not so much seek

To be consoled as to console;

To be understood as to understand;

To be loved as to love.

For it is in giving that we receive;

It is in pardoning that we are pardoned;

And it is in dying that we are born to eternal life.

THE LAW OF RELATIVITY

Perspective-taking encourages you to work on effective conflict resolutions for growth and learning. Gaining the skills required for shifting your focus and seeing issues from your partner's perspective promotes the discovery of uncovering erroneous beliefs and underlying causes of pattern conflict, such as unmet needs, past experiences, or differing values. Practicing self-development and couples' exercises encourages you to gain new understandings. It allows you to address the conflict's root causes rather than the surface-level symptoms.

Practicing perspective-taking requires intentional effort and mindfulness. You acquire skills through active listening, paraphrasing your partner's responses to ensure understanding, reframing negative assumptions, and eliminating judgment or criticism. You further your skills by actively practicing them by setting aside dedicated time for empathetic conversations to create a safe space for sharing and replacing old, broken foundational relationship blocks.

The skills and usage of perspective-taking promote unity and partnership within your relationship. By recognizing that your actions and words can have rippling effects on your partner and the relationship, you manage conflicts with greater care and consideration. This shifts the focus from winning arguments to finding mutually beneficial solutions that honor both partners' needs and desires. Beyond conflict resolution, perspective-taking can also lead to improved emotional connection and personal growth. You and your partner strengthen the bond to nurture a thriving, fully satisfying relationship where honor, respect, and appreciation are evident. It's possible! Keep reading and applying the laws.

∞∞∞∞

Another aspect of the Law of Relativity in relationship dynamics is the recognition that challenges often serve as opportunities for growth and transformation. Instead of viewing your relationship challenges as overwhelming obstacles, you can choose to see them as temporary setbacks, opportunities for growth, or projects for creative problem-solving. This shift in perspective encourages you to approach challenges with optimism, flexibility, and a sense of shared purpose. No matter how long you've been together - whether it's 2 years or 200 - treat your relationship like it's in its infancy. Actively seek ways to address issues delicately to avoid causing any undue harm.

For example, if one partner feels neglected due to the other's busy schedule, they can reframe this as an opportunity to communicate their needs and find a balance that works for both of them. By reframing challenges as learning experiences, you can approach them with curiosity and strength. Using each partner's strengths to seek and offer solutions that may have been previously overlooked or not considered. Think different to be different. Conflicts provide insights into underlying needs, communication patterns, and areas for personal development. Reframe to go with the flow, not against it.

In essence, the Law of Relativity stresses the importance of empathy and compassion in comprehending the relativeness of human experiences. Empathy is the basis of meaningful relationships. It allows you to validate each other's emotions and experiences. You develop an ability to empathize by engaging in the recommended tools and techniques within this book.

THE LAW OF RELATIVITY

Active listening is one of the initial skills needed for building empathy. This exercise encourages you to focus entirely on your partner and what they say without interruption or judgment. Start by making eye contact and giving your partner your full attention. Then, paraphrase what they've said to ensure you understand correctly and reflect on their emotions to show that you're engaged. Avoid jumping in with your perspective or solutions; instead, strive to listen with an open heart and mind.

Benefits aka What's in it for me

- Active listening helps you understand your partner's perspective more clearly, reducing misunderstandings and fostering more meaningful conversations.
- By fully focusing on what your partner is saying, you can better appreciate their feelings and experiences, enhancing your ability to empathize.
- When your partner feels heard and understood, it strengthens your emotional bond, leading to greater intimacy and trust.
- Active listening facilitates more effective conflict resolution by ensuring that both parties feel respected and valued, making it easier to find common ground.
- Consistently practicing active listening builds trust, demonstrating your commitment to valuing and understanding your partner's thoughts and feelings.
- Developing active listening skills can improve your overall communication abilities, benefiting not just your intimate relationships but also your interactions in other areas of life.

- Active listening can help alleviate the stress and tension that often arise from misunderstandings and unresolved conflicts by promoting direct and sincere communication.
- Active listening encourages mutual respect, as it involves giving your full attention and consideration to your partner, reinforcing the importance of their views and experiences.
- With a clearer understanding of each other's perspectives, you and your partner can make more informed and balanced decisions together.
- When both partners feel heard and understood, overall relationship satisfaction tends to increase, leading to a more fulfilling and joyous partnership.

Active listening is a building block of empathetic communication. Practice active listening by taking turns sharing a personal story or experience with your partner. While one person speaks, the other listens attentively without interrupting or offering advice. Afterward, switch roles and reflect back on what you heard, demonstrating understanding and empathy.

Perspective-Taking

Perspective-taking involves seeing the world, challenges, and issues from your partner's perspective. This exercise encourages you to set aside your own biases and preconceptions and imagine what it must be like to be in their situation. Asking open-ended questions without judgment can help you gain insight into your partner's thoughts, feelings, and beliefs. By actively seeking to understand your partner's perspective, you can develop empathy and compassion in your relationship, creating a space where both of you feel heard and valued.

Benefits aka What's in it for me

- Understanding others' perspectives allows you to empathize with their feelings and experiences, creating a deeper emotional connection.
- When you consider others' viewpoints, you can communicate more effectively, addressing their concerns and needs more accurately.
- Perspective-taking helps in resolving conflicts by enabling you to see the situation from multiple angles, facilitating cooperation and individual strengths.
- By valuing and understanding others' perspectives, you build trust and respect, which strengthens personal and professional relationships.
- Practicing perspective-taking reduces prejudices and biases, promoting a more inclusive and open-minded approach to situations.
- Considering different viewpoints leads to more creative and comprehensive solutions, as you can integrate various perspectives into your problem-solving process.
- Perspective-taking enhances your emotional intelligence by improving your ability to understand and manage your emotions and those of others.
- Understanding others' viewpoints improves patience and tolerance, as you appreciate the complexity of different experiences and opinions.

- ➢ Perspective-taking encourages self-reflection and personal growth, as you continually challenge your own assumptions and expand your knowledge.
- ➢ Practicing perspective-taking improves your social skills, making you more approachable, understanding, and relatable.

Set aside time with your partner to discuss a recent disagreement or challenge. After thoroughly examining the issue to understand it better and without raising emotions or conflict, take turns elaborating on it from both perspectives. Encourage each other to articulate each person's thoughts, feelings, and underlying needs without judgment. This exercise helps you recognize the relativity of experiences and gain insight into each other's viewpoints, decisions, and actions.

Practicing Compassion

This exercise involves extending kindness and understanding to your partner, especially during times of difficulty or conflict. Rather than reacting with anger or defensiveness, attempt to respond with empathy and care. Show genuine concern for your partner's well-being and offer support and encouragement when needed, regardless of your perception of who is right or wrong. By practicing compassion consistently, you can create an environment where both of you can express yourselves freely, knowing you are supported and loved. Where you feel valued and cared for, reestablishing emotional connection.

Benefits aka What's in it for me

- Compassion fosters deeper connections and trust in relationships, making interactions more meaningful and supportive.
- Showing compassion can lead to increased feelings of happiness, fulfillment, and overall emotional well-being.
- Compassionate behavior lowers stress levels by promoting positive emotions and reducing the impact of negative feelings.
- Practicing compassion enhances your ability to understand and share the feelings of others, improving your empathetic skills.
- Compassion helps resolve conflicts more effectively by promoting understanding and cooperation instead of hostility.
- Compassionate individuals often experience lower rates of depression and anxiety, contributing to gratitude and better mental health.
- Compassion builds emotional resilience, enabling you to cope better with personal challenges and setbacks.
- Acting with compassion can inspire others to do the same, creating an effect that promotes kindness and empathy within your relationship.
- Compassionate actions can give you a greater sense of purpose and meaning in life as you contribute positively to the well-being of yourself and others.
- Compassion has been linked to various physical health benefits, such as lower blood pressure, reduced inflammation, and a stronger immune system.

Discuss ways in which you can enhance compassion in your relationship. Give scenarios and examples of how you and your partner can develop the art of compassion together. Practicing compassion not only enriches your life but also positively impacts the lives of those around you, creating a more empathetic, understanding, and supportive world.

Role-Playing Scenarios

Engage in role-playing scenarios to practice empathetic responses to common relationship challenges. For instance, you could take turns portraying different perspectives within a hypothetical situation, such as disagreements over household chores or financial decisions. Avoid situations or conflicts that may still be sensitive in nature, take baby steps.

Benefits aka What's in it for me

- Role-playing allows you to practice and refine your verbal and non-verbal communication skills in a safe environment.
- It encourages creative thinking and helps you develop strategies for tackling real-life challenges.
- By taking on different roles, you gain insight into others' perspectives, fostering greater empathy and understanding.
- Regular practice in a controlled setting boosts your confidence in handling similar situations in real life.
- Role-playing helps you practice resolving conflicts effectively, enhancing your ability to manage disputes in real-life interactions.

- It fosters collaboration and teamwork, as participants must work together and understand each other's roles and perspectives.
- You gain a deeper understanding of your own behaviors and reactions, helping you to improve self-awareness and personal growth.
- Role-playing provides a safe space to make mistakes and learn from them without real-world consequences.
- It helps you develop the ability to adapt to different situations and respond flexibly to unexpected challenges.
- Engaging in role-playing scenarios helps reinforce learning and improves memory retention by providing practical, hands-on experience.

Practice responding with empathy, validation, and patience, even when faced with differing viewpoints. This exercise helps couples develop empathy by stepping into each other's shoes and exploring alternative perspectives.

Reflective Questioning

Use reflective questioning to encourage each other to share and expound on personal thoughts, feelings, and experiences by asking open-ended questions for deeper understanding.

Benefits aka What's in it for me

- ➢ Reflective questioning helps you gain a better understanding of your thoughts, feelings, and behaviors, leading to greater self-awareness.
- ➢ It encourages you to analyze and evaluate situations more deeply, enhancing your critical thinking skills.
- ➢ By examining different perspectives and underlying issues, reflective questioning can lead to more effective problem-solving.
- ➢ This practice helps you recognize and understand your emotions and those of others, contributing to higher emotional intelligence.
- ➢ Reflective questioning can foster empathy by encouraging you to consider others' viewpoints and experiences.
- ➢ It promotes thoughtful and informed decision-making by encouraging you to consider all aspects of a situation.
- ➢ Reflective questioning supports continuous personal development by challenging you to reflect on past experiences and learn from them.
- ➢ It helps you articulate your thoughts and feelings more clearly, leading to better communication with others.
- ➢ By reflecting on your actions and their consequences, you become more accountable for your behavior and decisions.
- ➢ Reflective questioning fosters deeper, more meaningful conversations, strengthening your relationships with others.

For example, instead of asking, "Why are you upset?" try asking, "Can you tell me more about what you're feeling and why?" This approach promotes empathy by inviting deeper exploration and validation of each other's emotions.

∞∞∞

Practical Applications for Conscious Living

These practical applications for conscious living are not just for you and your partner; they can enhance all areas of your life. Implementing these principles can improve family dynamics, establish better relationships with in-laws, and create harmony within biological and blended families. Parents, coworkers, and colleagues can also benefit from your conscious efforts, leading to more productive and positive interactions. By applying these practices, you create a domino effect that influences anyone who is a part of your life, creating a supportive and nurturing environment wherever you go.

Mindful Reflection

Establish mindfulness in reflecting on your experiences. Consider how challenges relate to the larger part of your life and their impact.

Benefits aka What's in it for me

➢ Mindful reflection helps you gain insights into your thoughts, emotions, and behaviors, leading to greater self-understanding.

- By focusing on the present moment and acknowledging your thoughts and feelings without judgment, mindful reflection can significantly reduce stress and anxiety.
- It helps you become more aware of your emotional responses, allowing you to manage and regulate your emotions more effectively.
- With increased clarity and awareness, mindful reflection promotes more thoughtful and informed decision-making.
- It encourages a deeper analysis of problems and challenges, leading to more effective and creative solutions.
- Practicing mindfulness improves your ability to concentrate and stay focused on tasks, enhancing productivity.
- Mindful reflection builds resilience by helping you develop a balanced perspective on challenges and setbacks.
- By fostering empathy and better communication, mindful reflection can strengthen your relationships with others.
- It supports continuous self-improvement and personal development by encouraging you to learn from past experiences.

Overall, mindful reflection contributes to a greater sense of peace, contentment, and well-being by promoting a balanced and mindful approach to life.

Perspective shifting

A practice that involves intentionally shifting your perspective on challenges. For example, you could explore alternative viewpoints highlighting the potential for growth, learning, and positive transformation. This practice can help you and your partner develop a more empathetic understanding of each other's experiences, backgrounds, beliefs, and perspectives, encouraging connection.

Benefits aka What's in it for me

- ➤ By understanding others' perspectives, you develop a deeper sense of empathy, improving your ability to connect with and support others.
- ➤ Viewing problems from multiple angles can lead to more innovative and effective solutions.
- ➤ Perspective shifting helps you understand the root causes of conflicts, making it easier to find mutually agreeable solutions.
- ➤ Embracing different viewpoints fosters open-mindedness and reduces biases and prejudices.
- ➤ By appreciating and respecting others' perspectives, you build stronger, more trusting relationships.
- ➤ Understanding different viewpoints improves your ability to communicate effectively and clearly.
- ➤ Perspective shifting enhances your ability to recognize and manage your own emotions and those of others.
- ➤ Viewing situations from different angles encourages continuous learning and personal development.

- Being able to see challenges from various perspectives helps you adapt and bounce back more effectively from setbacks.

Expanding your perspective helps you develop a more comprehensive and nuanced understanding of the world.

Empathy and Understanding

Approach your partner and others with compassion and understanding, recognizing the relativity of their experiences, traumas, culture, and beliefs. This practice supplements compassionate connections and enriches the connectedness of human relationships.

Benefits aka What's in it for me

- Empathy improves connections by allowing you to relate to and support others, building trust and intimacy in relationships.
- Understanding others' feelings and perspectives enhances your ability to communicate effectively, reducing misunderstandings.
- Empathetic understanding helps in resolving conflicts amicably by recognizing and addressing the concerns of all parties involved.
- Developing empathy improves your emotional intelligence, helping you manage your emotions and respond appropriately to others.
- Empathy leads to greater compassion and kindness, encouraging you to act in ways that support and uplift others.

- Understanding diverse perspectives enables more comprehensive and creative solutions to problems.
- In professional settings, empathy enables a collaborative and supportive work environment, enhancing teamwork and productivity.
- Practicing empathy encourages self-reflection and personal development, leading to a more profound understanding of yourself and others.
- Empathizing with others can reduce stress and anxiety.

Studies have shown that empathetic relationships can lead to better mental and physical health outcomes, promoting overall well-being.

Gratitude Practice

Incorporate gratitude practices into your daily routine. Express gratitude not only for the positive aspects of your life but also for the lessons and growth that challenges bring. This practice, when embraced, can help you acknowledge the place of challenges within the spectrum of relativity, promoting a sense of appreciation and mindfulness in your relationship journey.

Benefits aka What's in it for me
- Regularly practicing gratitude reduces symptoms of depression and anxiety, promoting a more positive outlook on life and challenges.

MANIFEST A JOY-FILLED RELATIONSHIP

- People who practice gratitude tend to exercise more, have fewer aches and pains, and report feeling healthier overall.
- Gratitude can improve sleep quality and duration by reducing negative thoughts and promoting a sense of peace.
- Focusing on what you're thankful for helps build resilience, allowing you to cope better with stress and adversity.
- Expressing gratitude to others strengthens relationships and encourages mutual support and kindness.
- Gratitude reduces social comparisons and builds appreciation for what you have, boosting your self-esteem and confidence.
- Practicing gratitude increases positive emotions like joy, happiness, and contentment, making you feel more fulfilled and satisfied.
- Grateful people tend to be more empathetic and less aggressive, contributing to a more harmonious and understanding social environment.
- Gratitude practice promotes mindfulness by encouraging you to be present and appreciate the current moment and the positive aspects of your life.
- Reflecting on what you are grateful for can give you a clearer sense of purpose and direction, motivating you to pursue meaningful goals and aspirations.

Incorporating these exercises into your relationship practice develops your ability to empathize and strengthens your emotional connection. By accepting the principles of the law, you can find new ways to combat old challenges with greater understanding, compassion, mutual support, and ease, reinforcing your bond and connection.

∞∞∞

By now, it should be evident that the Law of Relativity declares that nothing is inherently good or bad, but your perception and comparison give it meaning. This principle is influential in developing gratitude, especially when combined with the imaginative faculties of your mind. Shifting your perspective and using your imagination can transform your outlook and induce a deeper sense of gratitude.

Research on the psychology of gratitude illustrates how embracing a grateful mindset can improve your well-being and satisfaction. By understanding the principles of relativity, you can become more aware of how your experiences are subjective. This awareness is fundamental to personal development and improving your relationship dynamics.

Challenges take on a different significance when viewed in relation to the blessings and opportunities present in your life. Imagine a puzzle with light and dark pieces; the contrast enhances the beauty of the whole picture. Likewise, gratitude in adversity becomes a force that alters your perception of challenges, accentuating the richness and complexity of your life experiences.

Your imagination is a powerful tool that can assist you in manifesting a joy-filled relationship by helping you see the beauty of what you have, irrespective of what you think is missing. It lets you see beyond the current reality and create a picture of your true desires. By using your imagination, you can shape, form, and give color to all aspects of your relationship, transforming your perspective and enhancing your appreciation for your partner.

Imagination is the universal spectrum of endless possibilities for your happiness. It enables you to envision the good you desire and see it clearly in your mind, even before it becomes reality. By combining gratitude with imagination, you can vividly picture your relational goals and aspirations, bringing them closer to fruition. This mental visualization and reframing help you appreciate what you have and motivates you to manifest your deepest desires through the Law of Relativity.

The mind power of your imagination can reshape your perception of your reality. By actively imagining different scenarios and perspectives, you can shift your focus from what is lacking to what is abundant in your life. Here's how you can use your imagination to harness the Law of Relativity and enhance gratitude.

Imagine Alternative Scenarios

Picture how your life could be different under less fortunate circumstances. For instance, imagine having fewer resources, opportunities, or health. This comparison can make you more appreciative of what you currently have.

Visualize Positive Outcomes

When faced with a challenge, imagine the potential positive outcomes. Visualize how overcoming this obstacle could lead to growth and new opportunities. This shift in focus helps you see difficulties as steppingstones rather than setbacks.

THE LAW OF RELATIVITY

Compare Past and Present

Reflect on past struggles and compare them to your current situation. Recognize the progress you have made and the lessons you have learned. This retrospective view can raise gratitude for your growth and resilience.

Envision the Bigger Picture

Use your imagination to step back and see the larger picture of your life. Understand how various experiences, both good and bad, contribute to your overall journey. This holistic view can help you appreciate the interconnectedness of all events.

By applying the Law of Relativity and harnessing the power of your imagination, you can transform your perspective and develop a profound sense of gratitude. This shift in focus allows you to see the abundance in your life, appreciate the positive aspects of your experiences, and create a more fulfilling existence. Embrace this practice and watch as your life becomes enriched with a deeper appreciation for the present moment and all it holds.

∞∞∞

Improve gratitude by focusing on the positive aspects of your relationship and appreciating the support, love, and companionship you share. Regularly remind yourself of the moments of joy and connection that outweigh the temporary struggles. This practice helps you maintain a balanced perspective and reinforces your emotional resilience. Thoughts held in mind produce after it's kind. Keep positive thoughts to produce positive outcomes.

Practices/Strategies for Building Emotional Resilience

Shifting your perspective is one of the most powerful strategies for building emotional resilience in your relationship. The Law of Relativity teaches us that our experiences gain meaning through our limited awareness based on comparisons. For instance, when faced with a disagreement, you can reframe your perspective by considering how the situation could be worse or how you have overcome similar obstacles. This perspective shift helps you contextualize your challenges and build a sense of gratitude for the positives in your relationship. You are opening up the opportunity to work through conflicts together, viewing the issues more positively.

Gratitude is a powerful tool for fortifying emotional resilience in your relationship. Focusing on the positive aspects of your relationship can bolster your resilience in the face of challenges. The Law of Relativity reminds us that everything is relative, and by practicing gratitude, you're shifting your focus away from your problems and towards the strengths and blessings in your relationship. Whether it's through a gratitude journal or regular expressions of appreciation, cultivating gratitude can help you maintain a positive outlook.

Communication is vital for building emotional resilience in your relationship. You can enhance your resilience by practicing open, honest, and empathetic communication. This involves actively listening to each other's concerns without interrupting or forcing your position, validating each other's feelings even if you can't relate or don't fully understand, and expressing compassion and a willingness to understand and resolve issues that end in a win-win scenario – you both win, and the relationship wins. By communicating effectively, you acquire the skills to overcome challenges together and strengthen your communication. For example, setting aside dedicated time for communication to openly express your feelings using 'I' statements and practicing active listening contribute to effective communication in your relationship.

In this context, flexibility refers to the ability to adapt to changing circumstances and handle challenges to maintain the health and stability of your relationship. This involves accepting each other's way of handling things, working through and finding creative solutions to problems, and letting go of unrealistic, unmet expectations. Improving your flexibility allows you to weather the storms of life and maintain a strong and resilient relationship.

Recognize the importance of setting and respecting healthy boundaries to maintain your emotional well-being and preserve the integrity of your relationship. Have open discussions about your individual needs, preferences, and boundaries, and assertively communicate and uphold these boundaries with each other.

Benefits

- ❖ Clear boundaries build trust, as both partners understand and respect each other's limits.

- ❖ Open discussions about needs and preferences lead to better communication.

- ❖ Establishing and upholding boundaries establishes respect and consideration.

- ❖ Boundaries create a safe space for expressing emotions without fear of judgment or overstepping.

- ❖ Clear boundaries help prevent misunderstandings and conflicts.

- ❖ Respecting each other's boundaries encourages individual growth and self-discovery.

- ❖ Boundaries allow each partner to maintain their independence while nurturing the relationship.

- ❖ Knowing and setting boundaries are for you, not your partner.

- ❖ Boundaries ensure that dependency in the relationship remains healthy and not overbearing.

- ❖ Establishing and adhering to boundaries contributes to the long-term stability and success of the relationship.

The Law of Relativity offers valuable insights into building emotional resilience within marriage and intimate relationships. By shifting perspectives, practicing gratitude, communicating effectively, refining flexibility, and establishing healthy boundaries, you are applying the principles of relativity to your relationship. For instance, shifting perspectives and practicing gratitude help you see your relationship in a more positive light, while effective communication and flexibility allow you to adapt and respond to challenges in a way that strengthens your relationship. Drawing upon the principles of relativity, you learn to look differently into other options and views you may have never considered before. You are elevating your consciousness to different ways of thinking in overcoming and strengthening your bond and building a relationship that withstands the tests of time.

∞∞∞

In the intricate affairs of marriage and intimate relationships, the Law of Relativity, a principle derived from physics, guides you into seeing things from a different perspective. It suggests that the way you perceive things is not absolute, but rather, it depends on the circumstances and the relationship between the elements involved. This means your understanding of a situation can change when you consider it in relation to other aspects of your relationship. Understanding and applying the law helps bridge the gap in building resilience in the face of relational challenges. These shared stories of overcoming challenges through a relative perspective illustrate the power of this principle in aiding resilience within relationships.

Consider Jordan and LaMia, who faced a significant financial setback early in their relationship. At first, LaMia felt overwhelmed and defeated by their circumstances, while Jordan remained optimistic and focused on finding solutions. However, by applying the Law of Relativity, LaMia shifted her perspective. She recognized that while their financial situation was challenging, they were fortunate to have each other's support and love. Viewing their challenges in relation to others who may be facing even greater hardships helped LaMia gain gratitude for the positives. This shift in perspective empowered LaMia and Jordan to face their financial and other relational difficulties with resilience and determination, ultimately strengthening their bond as they worked together to overcome obstacles.

Consider the journey of Patric and Michelle, who navigated a period of strained communication and conflict in their relationship. Patric and Michelle were caught in a cycle of blame and resentment as tensions mounted. However, by applying the Law of Relativity, they began to view their conflicts in relation to the broader context of their relationship. They recognized that their disagreements were a natural part of being in a committed partnership and that they had overcome challenges together in the past. This relative perspective not only helped Patric and Michelle approach their conflicts with greater compassion and understanding but also empowered them to take control of their relationship, leading to more constructive conversations.

Stories have the power to inspire, offering glimpses into the triumphs and tribulations of real-life relationships. By sharing these stories of couples who have overcome challenges through a relative perspective, we believe you will draw inspiration and reassurance that you, too, can navigate your difficulties with courage and resilience. We also invite you to share your own stories of how you've applied the Law of Relativity in your relationship. These stories serve as beacons of hope, reminding us that adversity can be transformed into an opportunity for growth and building stronger connections when approached with empathy and understanding.

THE LAW OF RELATIVITY

Discuss with your partner how these lessons offer practical guidance and can be applied to your own life and relationship for inspiration in overcoming your challenges.

Reflect on the stories shared and consider how they relate to your own experiences and struggles. We strongly encourage you to engage in open dialogue and introspection to identify areas where you can apply the principles of relativity, empathy, and resilience to strengthen your relationship.

The transformative power of adopting a relative perspective and building emotional resilience means the ability to bounce back from challenges and maintain a positive emotional connection. It is not what happens to us but how we perceive the act. If our focus is negative, we will be influenced to see things as negative. On the other hand, if we believe everything comes to help us grow or benefit our lives somehow, then our perception will help influence our experiences as positive. Practice seeing challenges as channels for positive change and approaching them with courage, compassion, and determination to overcome them together.

In *The Revealing Word* by Charles Fillmore (Martino Publishing, 2014), the definition of "perception, spiritual" states, "the faculty of seeing spiritual reality in spite of appearances that may suggest the contrary."

Chapter Ten
THE LAW OF POLARITY
Balancing Duality in Relationships

The Law of Polarity proposes that every aspect of existence possesses its opposite, forming a continuum of polarities that shape your reality. Understanding and embracing polarities becomes necessary for working through differences, encouraging complementarity, and developing a holistic connection. Understanding the dynamic interaction between opposites creates balance and harmony in your relationship.

At the heart of your relationship lies a delicate ball of energies - the Law of Polarity in action. This fundamental principle, drawn from the realms of physics and philosophy, offers insights into the power and complexity of your human connections, particularly within your relationship. It manifests through the dynamic interaction of you and your partner's energies, creating a nest of contrasts and complements.

The Law of Polarity contends that opposites are interconnected and complementary. This concept includes day and night, light and dark, love and fear, joy and sorrow; one cannot exist without the other. Challenges are natural, but within them lies the potential for progression and transformation. Every challenge you experience holds the seed of possibility, and every shadow offers the potential for light, reassuring you of the balance and harmony in your relationship.

Therefore, in your relationship journey, you and your partner will encounter a range of experiences - highs and lows, joys and challenges. The Law of Polarity teaches you that these opposing forces are not contradictory but complementary. Accepting these polarities allows you to overcome challenges with a sense of unity. Recognizing that relational growth often emerges from adversity, you and your partner approach difficulties with a shared insight.

∞∞∞

Research on tension and resolution in relational dynamics highlights you and your partner's active role in the transformative potential of polarities. Psychological studies on personality differences and compatibility offer insights into how individuals with contrasting traits can complement each other within relationships.

Your polarity contributes to the depth of your relationships through the principle of attraction. This means that you are naturally drawn to partners who exhibit qualities that complement your own. Just like magnets, you are often drawn to those who embody traits you admire or desire. For example, a person with a strong, assertive nature may find themselves irresistibly drawn to someone who exudes warmth and nurturing qualities. This attraction creates a sense of balance and accord as each of you brings something unique to the relationship. As the relationship grows, you may find yourself starting to emulate or imitate the opposing qualities of your partner. Sometimes, this brings balance, and sometimes, it brings tension.

Challenges may arise when you start to dislike the same attributes you once admired. By examining the principles of polarity, you see how you and your partner's yin and yang shape your connection. You establish a natural balance that creates synergy when you accept your complementary roles.

The Law of Polarity also shows up as a potential for conflict and pull when you fail to support your complementary roles. If one partner dominates while the other suppresses their authentic nature, imbalance and resentment arise. For instance, consistently exhibiting dominant traits while your partner suppresses their desires and opinions leads to frustration – or vice versa. This imbalance causes feelings of disconnect between you and your partner, which can persist for years without either of you understanding why. This frustration and imbalance pose significant challenges if not carefully addressed. When you try to fix the imbalance out of frustration, your relationship becomes a battleground. However, correctly understanding how to overcome these challenges gives you a better chance of strengthening the relationship than destroying it. You cannot solve your problems at the level they were created; you must rise above them. Suppose you do not seek help to rectify your relationship challenges beyond your current level of understanding. In that case, you are doing more harm than good.

Relationship polarities contribute to the fruitfulness of your connection through synergy and collaboration. You propel your relationship forward when you learn to recognize, work on, and welcome your opposite traits. You ensure that each partner's strengths and weaknesses complement one another, creating a sense of wholeness and completeness that transcends individual limitations.

THE LAW OF POLARITY

"You complete me." - Jerry Maguire

This famous movie line captures the essence of the Law of Polarity in relationships. It emphasizes the idea that differences and polarities contribute to a partnership's completeness. By embracing and valuing the unique qualities you and your partner bring, you create a relationship that is greater than the sum of its parts.

Acknowledging and honoring the full spectrum of each other's nature creates space for authenticity and vulnerability, building emotional intimacy and trust. Leverage your polarities by improving open communication, extending compassion, and showing mutual respect. Develop practical skills to converse honestly about your needs, desires, and boundaries.

∞∞∞

The concept of conscious coupling becomes a focal point, encouraging you to handle differences with intention and awareness. Practical strategies and techniques for effective communication, such as non-defensive listening and negotiation, offer tools for understanding and handling contrasting perspectives and polarities.

Practical strategies for applying the Law of Polarity in your relationship involve developing self-awareness, gaining effective communication skills for open communication, and reestablishing mutual respect. You learn to accept and engage in honest conversations about your needs, desires, and expectations, allowing space for both energies to thrive.

Practical Insight: Engaging in direct and honest communication is crucial during challenging times. Try to avoid withdrawal and seclusion. Acknowledge your differences and actively seek common ground. Recognize that the challenges you encounter present opportunities for relational and mutual growth. Challenges show you where you need more skills to manifest your desired relationship. They become obstacles that can make or break you when overlooked and ignored. Manifesting is about becoming a conscious creator in the universe, not leaving it up to universal chance.

Yet, the actual innate value of your relationship lies in transforming these polarities into complementary forces for love, expansion, and fulfillment. Here, we offer practical strategies and tools for integrating and balancing polarities.

The journey towards integration begins with self-awareness. We encourage each partner to reflect on their own strengths, weaknesses, and tendencies. Identify the dominant energies within yourself and acknowledge how they manifest in thoughts, emotions, and behaviors. Recognizing these patterns lays the foundation for understanding and joining the complementary energies present within your relationship.

Authenticity is the foundation of a balanced relationship. We encourage you to accept and value your true self without conforming to societal expectations or gender stereotypes. Create a safe space for vulnerability and expression where you and your partner feel accepted and valued for who you are. By honoring authenticity, you pave the way for the integration of polarities, allowing for a more genuine and intimate connection.

Effective communication is key for balancing the complexities of polarities within your relationship. Engage in open, honest dialogues about your needs, desires, and boundaries.

Understand that being able to express those things to your partner leaves little room for false beliefs or assumptions. Adopt a culture of active listening and seeing things from your partner's awareness, where both partners feel heard and understood. By communicating openly, you begin to bridge the gap between your differences and find common ground for integration.

Empathy is the bridge that connects you across your differences. We encourage you to improve empathy by putting yourself in each other's shoes and seeking to understand your different perspectives. By empathizing with one another's experiences, you transcend your individual viewpoint and forge emotional connections based on maturity and mutual understanding.

Respect is the backbone of a healthy relationship. Focus on adopting an attitude of appreciation for each other's unique strengths and contributions, regardless of gender or role. Celebrate the diversity of your perspectives and approaches that each partner brings to the relationship. By valuing each other's differences, you lay the groundwork for a balanced combination of polarities.

Collaboration is essential to integrating polarities. Remember to work together as a team, leveraging each other's strengths to overcome challenges and achieve shared goals. This may seem like a no-brainer; however, in the midst of anger and emotions, teamwork is usually the last thing you are thinking. Envelop a spirit of cooperation and flexibility, where you are willing to meet on mutual ground and make concessions for the greater good of the relationship. By embracing collaboration and cooperation, you strengthen unity and synergy that transcends your differences.

Transforming polarities into complementary forces is a journey of self-discovery, empathy, and collaboration. By cultivating self-awareness, embracing authenticity, and practicing open communication, you lay and reinforce the foundation for successfully integrating and enhancing your natural polarities. As polarities merge and complement each other, your relationship will blossom into a vibrant bouquet of unconditional love, lasting happiness, and endless joy. Don't take our word for it, try it yourself! Let us know by reaching out to us at connect@legendaryrelationship.com.

By accepting and leveraging the natural polarities within your partnership, you unlock many benefits that contribute to your evolution and relationship satisfaction.

∞∞∞∞

The Law of Polarity challenges you to transcend judgment and appreciate the neutrality inherent in dualities. The law emphasizes unity within diversity and acknowledges that opposites are integral parts of the whole. Picture a mosaic where contrasting tiles contribute to the intricate beauty of the artwork. Similarly, life's mosaic is enriched by the diversity of your experiences, perspectives, and emotions. Recognizing the unity within the beauty of dualities allows you to release judgment and view your contrasting traits without attaching labels of good or bad, positive or negative. It builds a sense of interconnectedness, inviting you to celebrate the multiplicity of your existence. In this neutrality, you discover the freedom to direct the flow of polarities with greater ease and wisdom.

The dynamic interaction of polarities within your relationship serves as a stimulus for personal development and growth. You are challenged to confront your own limitations, prejudices, and insecurities, encouraging self-reflection and introspection. By embracing discomfort and uncertainty, you expand your awareness and develop a greater desire for understanding. Stepping outside your comfort zone allows you to see new perspectives and understand your partner more deeply. Facing uncertainties together helps you grow individually and as a couple. Approaching challenges with an open heart, you learn to be more patient, empathetic, and understanding, enhancing the overall quality of your relationship.

When you become aware, your perspective changes, leading to new ways of seeing and doing things. Awareness brings a shift in understanding, enabling you to recognize patterns and behaviors that may have been previously overlooked. This heightened awareness encourages you to question assumptions and beliefs that shape your interactions and decisions.

As your perspective broadens, you start seeing situations from different angles, fostering empathy and compassion. You become more attuned to your partner's needs, emotions, and viewpoints. This change in perspective allows you to approach conflicts with a mindset focused on resolution rather than blame.

Awareness also empowers you to make conscious choices. Instead of reacting impulsively, you can respond thoughtfully, considering the impact of your actions on your partner and the relationship as a whole. You start practicing active listening, showing genuine interest in your partner's experiences, and communicating more effectively.

This transformation extends to your actions as well. With a new perspective, you may adopt healthier habits, engage in activities that promote mutual growth, and prioritize quality time together. You become more mindful of the small gestures that contribute to your partner's happiness, strengthening your emotional connection.

Becoming aware and changing your perspective enriches your relationship. It creates a positive cycle of growth and love where you and your partner feel valued, heard, and supported. Your awareness helps you see how your and your partner's unique perspectives enrich the collective dialogue.

The fusion of polarities within your relationship sparks creativity and innovation. Your different perspectives and approaches inspire you to explore new possibilities and envision a future that is rich with potential. By accepting diversity and accepting change, you co-create a relationship that is vibrant, dynamic, and filled with endless possibilities. By welcoming your diverse viewpoints and experiences, you boost your appreciation for each other's differences, allowing desired relational manifestations to transpire. The universe is your canvas; paint your desires across the sky.

Practices/Techniques/Exercises for Conscious Living

Consciously develop mindful observation of dualities in your life. Notice how contrasting experiences, emotions, and perspectives contribute to the richness of your personal journey.

∞∞∞

Develop equanimity by releasing attachment to judgments of good or bad. Approach experiences with a sense of neutrality, recognizing their place within the dynamics of polarities.

When faced with challenges, engage in reflective practices to explore their transformative potential. Consider how each challenge leads to personal growth, flexibility, and the discovery of inner strengths.

Foster a sense of unity consciousness by recognizing the interconnectedness of all things. Appreciate the diversity within your own experiences and the collective human experience, embracing the oneness that underlies all things.

The yin and yang symbol embodies the essence of the Law of Polarity. Within the circle of unity, the black and white halves represent opposing forces in dynamic equilibrium. The small dots within each half signify the potential for transformation and the presence of the opposite within. This ancient symbol serves as a visual reminder of the interdependence and balance within dualities.

Self-Reflection and Awareness

Exercise: Take time individually to reflect on your own strengths, weaknesses, and tendencies. Journal about your dominant energies - masculine and feminine - and how they manifest in your thoughts, emotions, and behaviors.

Discussion: Share your reflections with your partner openly and non-judgmentally. Explore how your individual energies complement each other and contribute to the dynamics of the relationship.

Balancing Roles and Responsibilities

Redistribution of Tasks: Regularly review and redistribute household tasks, emotional labor, and decision-making responsibilities based on each partner's strengths, preferences, and workload.

Exercise: List household tasks, emotional labor, and decision-making responsibilities. Identify areas where one partner may be shouldering a disproportionate burden.

Action Plan: Work together to redistribute tasks and responsibilities in a fair and equitable way. Embrace flexibility and cooperation to ensure that both partners feel supported and valued in their contributions.

Embracing Vulnerability and Authenticity

Exercise: Set aside regular time for authentic sharing and vulnerability. Practice active listening and empathy as you share your thoughts, feelings, and fears with your partner.

Action Plan: Create a safe space for vulnerability within your relationship, free from judgment or criticism. Encourage each other to express emotions openly and honestly, fostering a deeper sense of connection and intimacy.

Cultivating Empathy and Understanding

Exercise: Take turns stepping into each other's shoes and seeing the world from their perspective. Practice active listening and empathy as you share your experiences and emotions.

Action Plan: Make a conscious effort to validate and empathize with your partner's feelings, even when disagreeing. Foster a culture of understanding and compassion within your relationship, strengthening your bond and connection.

Communication and Conflict Resolution

Constructive Conflict: Approach conflicts as opportunities for growth and understanding, rather than as battlegrounds for proving who is right or wrong.

Exercise: Practice active listening and constructive communication techniques during conflicts or disagreements. Use "I" statements to express your feelings and needs without blaming or criticizing your partner.

Action Plan: Develop a toolkit of healthy conflict resolution strategies, such as collaboration, negotiation, and problem-solving. Commit to resolving conflicts peacefully and respectfully, maintaining open lines of communication and understanding.

Cultivating Shared Hobbies and Interests

Exercise: Explore new activities and hobbies together that cater to both partners' interests and preferences. Whether it's cooking, hiking, or painting, find ways to connect and bond through shared experiences.

Action Plan: Schedule regular date nights or quality time together to engage in these shared activities. Celebrate each other's differences and embrace the joy of discovery and exploration as you deepen your connection.

Honoring Individual Needs and Boundaries

Exercise: Assess your individual needs, desires, and boundaries. Communicate these openly and honestly with your partner, respecting each other's individuality and choices.

Action Plan: Establish clear boundaries and agreements that honor each partner's needs and preferences. Practice mutual respect and consent in all aspects of your relationship, creating a safe and supportive environment for personal growth and fulfillment.

Finding and maintaining balance within marriage and intimate relationships requires intention, effort, and commitment from both partners. By embracing the Law of Polarity and engaging in practical exercises designed to promote balance, you create a relationship that is grounded, harmonious, and deeply fulfilling. Through self-reflection, empathy, communication, and shared experiences, partners navigate the complexities of polarities with grace and resilience, furthering a love that grows stronger with each passing day.

Embrace flexibility and adaptability in role expectations, recognizing that the division of labor may shift over time due to changing circumstances and life stages.

Adopt a practice of gratitude by regularly expressing appreciation for your partner's qualities, actions, and contributions to the relationship.

Communicate with kindness, respect, and empathy, even in moments of disagreement or conflict. Honor each other's boundaries, preferences, and independence.

THE LAW OF POLARITY

Encourage and support each other's personal growth and development goals, whether they involve career aspirations, hobbies, or self-development.

Approach your relationship as a journey of continuous learning and adaptation, recognizing that growth and refinement are ongoing processes.

Remain open to feedback, new ideas, and changes in circumstances, adapting your approach to relationship dynamics as needed to maintain harmony and balance.

Balancing and harmonizing polarities is an ongoing process that requires both partners' intention, effort, and commitment. When you integrate your complementary energies, you create a dynamic equilibrium of wholeness and completeness. This balance allows you to support and complement each other easily. Through all the above practices, you develop a relationship that is rooted in harmony by creating a holistic and synergistic partnership.

However, balance within the Law of Polarity is not static but dynamic. Imagine a tightrope walker adjusting their balance in response to external forces. Similarly, directing the dance of dualities involves continuous adjustment and adaptation, allowing you to maintain balance amid the ever-changing currents of life.

The Law of Polarity pushes you to seek the light within the darkness, recognizing your potential for growth and revelation. Within life's darkness lie opportunities for self-discovery and the unfolding of hidden potentials. You must trust that challenges carry the seeds of transformation revealing what lies

MANIFEST A JOY-FILLED RELATIONSHIP

within. Learning to embrace contrast enriches your experiences; challenging times help you appreciate the good ones; knowing what you don't want in your relationship sheds light on what you want, and rainy days make you cherish sunny days. As the saying goes, "To love your life, you can't hate the experiences that shaped you." Experiences, such as seeming failures or challenges, contribute to your growth and appreciation of your relationship's success.

From *What We Believe* by Don Nedd, commentary by Helen W. Carry, "We have to become consciously aware that the kingdom we seek is already within us. It is the essence of our very being and we have only to bring it into expression. It is not the material things (clothes, homes, cars, etc.) that we truly seek but rather the qualities that those things cause us to experience such as beauty, happiness, joy" (Nedd, 1990, p. 4).

Chapter Eleven
THE LAW OF RHYTHM
Recognizing and Adapting to the Natural Rhythms of Relationships

Life unfolds in cycles, much like the changing seasons. The Law of Rhythm emphasizes the importance of understanding and accepting these cycles, which shape the ebb and flow of love, intimacy, and connection. You can anticipate and prepare for the inevitable trials and tribulations by aligning with these rhythms. You are preparing for smoother transitions through life's fluctuations.

This principle shows you how everything in life moves in alternating waves of expansion and contraction, creation and destruction, or stability and change. Relating this law to your relationship helps you to transition with optimism through the ups and downs. Acknowledging relational conflict as part of a broader pattern enables you to journey together in reassurance as you build and shape your relationship through your awareness of this law. Understanding that every relationship goes through phases allows you to approach both the highs and lows with greater resilience and patience. Instead of being caught off guard by difficulties, you can view them as temporary and necessary parts of growth.

Studying this universal law gives you a broader perspective. It makes you aware of how rhythmic patterns shape your relational experiences. By reflecting on your knowledge and experiences, you identify periods of closeness, intimacy, and joy and times of distance, conflict, or stagnation. You can pinpoint when and where you encountered emotional highs that were succeeded by emotional lows and discover where periods of intense connection alternated with times of solitude or reflection.

Adapting to your relationship's natural rhythms can make transitioning easier. Recognizing that these changes are a natural and predictable aspect of your relationship journey is necessary for ensuring a more enduring partnership.

∞∞∞

You initiate the first step toward accepting and adapting to your relationship rhythms through your awareness of the law. By realizing that challenges and conflicts are not anomalies but integral parts of your relationship path, you can shift your perspective from problem-based to solution-based. You are empowered to navigate your relationship with strength and stability, enabling you and your partner to weather the storms together without fear of possible destruction. Unfortunately, as major life events happen, such as kids, careers, parents, empty nesters, etc., you may encounter cycles over and over again. Just as the tides rise and fall, your relationship undergoes fluctuations influenced by various negative and positive factors, internal and external circumstances, and individual and collective issues. By adapting to these rhythms, instead of becoming frustrated and resisting them, you can learn to steer your relationship through them successfully.

THE LAW OF RHYTHM

Like forming a team, your relationship follows natural cycles defined by the Law of Rhythm. When you first come together, you experience the excitement and novelty of the initial phase, much like a newly assembled team full of enthusiasm and potential. This phase, known as "forming," is characterized by enthusiasm, optimism, and a sense of possibility. Team members are polite and eager to make a good impression, just as you might be in the early stages of a relationship. During this time, your role is to facilitate introductions, establish common goals, and create a foundation of trust, much like the honeymoon phase, marked by high energy and a strong sense of connection, where everything seems possible.

As you settle into the routine, the initial excitement may fade, and you face the first challenges together. This phase mirrors the storming phase of team development, where differences in perspectives and working styles emerge. You might encounter conflicts, misunderstandings, or moments of distance in your relationship. It's essential to recognize that these challenges are a natural part of the rhythm, not signs of a failing relationship.

Moving forward, you enter a phase of norming, where you start to understand each other's strengths and weaknesses. You learn to appreciate the unique qualities your partner brings to the relationship. By aligning your energies and finding common ground, you begin to harmonize your differences, much like a team finding its groove. This period builds connection and mutual respect.

As you progress, you reach the performing stage, where your relationship functions smoothly and you feel a strong sense of partnership. You and your partner support each other through ups and downs, much like a well-coordinated team that works together seamlessly to achieve its goals. This phase is characterized by stability, confidence, and working well together.

However, even in the performing stage, rhythms continue to shift. Just as a team faces new projects or challenges, your relationship will encounter changes and transitions. Although you have tackled some issues successfully, the process begins all over again with each new challenge. Unfortunately, challenges don't come in one size. Some challenges stretch you well beyond your comfort zone. However, staying aware of these natural cycles allows you to approach each phase with persistence and flexibility. Identifying the ebb and flow of intimacy, you understand that moments of distance can lead to renewed closeness if navigated correctly with care.

To manage these cycles effectively, open communication, empathy, and adaptability must be practiced where you view your relationship challenges as opportunities for expansion and elevation. By aligning with the Law of Rhythm, you can maintain a balanced and loving relationship that thrives through collaboration and mutual support.

∞∞∞

By honoring the natural cycles of love, you recognize that your relationship will go through different phases, much like everything in life. There will be moments of intense intimacy as well as times of distance. It's not the ups and downs that matter, but how you react when they appear. Are you savoring the highs and rejecting the lows? Your goal in the relationship should be to strive for balance and understanding whenever these cycles arise.

THE LAW OF RHYTHM

Recognizing and respecting these cycles helps you build a strong foundation of trust, longevity, and mutual respect. You can easily maneuver the ups and downs by keeping the lines of communication open, adapting to change, and being mindful of your relationship's rhythms. This approach allows you to make meaningful progress together, regulate your reactions, and strengthen your bond in unimaginable ways.

However, you must gain communication skills to get you through these ups and downs successfully. Share your thoughts and feelings openly, listen and hear, and strive to understand each other's perspectives. Clear and truthful communication helps you stay connected and work through issues. Keeping the lines of communication open ensures that both partners feel appreciated and respected, essential for maintaining trust and intimacy. Effective communication allows you to address concerns before they escalate. By consistently engaging in meaningful dialogue, you create a supportive environment where you can succeed together. Strengthen communication skills by using the practices in this book alongside other tools and techniques found on our website, legendaryrelationship.com.

Relationships are full of unexpected twists and turns, and you will undoubtedly face different challenges and transitions. You can navigate these shifts by being flexible and willing to adjust to new circumstances. This means thinking and feeling greater than the challenges, shifting your perspective to see challenges as opportunities, and being aware of the intentions behind your words and actions during challenging times. When you adapt to changes, you show that you value your relationship enough to grow and evolve with it, confirming that you can overcome obstacles and continue to flourish together. Adaptability promotes effective communication by encouraging you to remain open-minded, receptive, and responsive to each other's needs and perspectives. Adapting to changes as a team leverages your ability to do it with your partner instead of against them. Remember, you and your partner are against the problem, not on opposite sides of the problem. By cultivating adaptability, you can guide the ins and outs of your relational dynamics with mindfulness, grace, self-control, and mutual self-development, establishing poise, patience, forgiveness, accountability, and bliss along your journey of love and happiness.

∞∞∞

Mindfulness always plays a vital role in maintaining a healthy relationship. Being mindful of your relationship's rhythms involves recognizing and honoring the natural cycles that occur within your partnership. Just as seasons change, so too will the dynamics of your relationship. Pay attention to your partner's needs and emotions, and be present in your interactions. This is equal to what you want and expect from them. This awareness guides your actions and reactions, allowing you to respond to each other with kindness, understanding, and, most of all, dignity.

Know that marriage and intimate relationships are not static entities but evolve continually. You are not the same person you were ten years ago, so why would you expect your partner or relationship to be? As you change in your natural cycle, so will your relationship.

THE LAW OF RHYTHM

You have experienced intense connection and passion, marked by mutual understanding, shared goals, and deep emotional intimacy. Only to have those moments of expansion followed by periods of contraction, during which challenges, conflicts, or external stressors strain the very essence of your union. Understanding these principles allows you to recognize predictable patterns shaping your relationship. Recognizing your rhythmic patterns enables you to make more conscious choices.

Discussing and working through the down periods and patterns are essential for successfully managing complexities, anticipating challenges, and adapting to adversity. By observing your individual relationship patterns, such as recurring themes and challenges, you can make intentional choices aligned with your relationship's highest purpose. While the cyclical nature of relational patterns may present challenges, it also offers opportunities for growth, transformation, and renewal. Just as the seasons transition from winter to spring, relationships undergo phases of renewal and rebirth. Couples who embrace these transitions with openness and wonder discover new depths of connection and intimacy, revitalizing their love and commitment in the process.

∞∞∞

The Law of Rhythm emphasizes the power of aligning your actions with the natural flow of your relationship. Picture a surfer catching a wave; their skill lies in harmonizing with the rhythm of the ocean. Similarly, when you align your intentions and actions with the inherent rhythm of your relationship, you will experience a sense of ease and synchronicity. This alignment becomes a guiding force, propelling you and your partner toward fulfilling your desired aspirations for your union.

However, this requires flexibility and adaptability. When you resist your relationship's natural cycles, you may be caught in a perpetual struggle against the tide. Knowing what you want doesn't make it happen. Instead, you can surrender to the flow through understanding and changing your thinking.

"Life is a series of natural and spontaneous changes. Don't resist them; that only creates sorrow. Let reality be reality. Let things flow naturally forward in whatever way they like." - Lao Tzu

Lao Tzu's wisdom sums up the essence of the Law of Rhythm. It encourages you to expect the inherent changes and cycles in life and your relationship by realizing that resistance only leads to distress. By allowing things to flow naturally, you can find peace and equilibrium within the dynamic rhythms of your intimate connections.

Practices/Techniques

- ❖ During challenging times, it is essential for you to remain anchored in your commitment to each other and your shared vision for your relationship.

- ❖ Develop mindfulness and attunement to your relationship's rhythms. Pay attention to subtle shifts in energy, mood, and dynamics. By staying present and observant, you can anticipate changes and respond proactively.

- ❖ Recognize your own emotional responses and triggers and strive to communicate them openly and honestly with your partner.

- Seek to understand your partner's perspective and emotions, even when they differ from your own. Empathy adds connection and mutual support during difficult times.

- Open the lines of communication with small challenges. Then, work your way up to sharing and listening to understand each other. Don't seek to be understood; seek to understand first and foremost. As you begin to feel comfortable reestablishing trust and security, you can intentionally create a safe and non-judgmental space for dialogue where both partners can feel comfortable expressing their thoughts, feelings, and needs without fear of them later resurfacing.

- Focus on maintaining emotional intimacy and connection, even amidst disagreements or challenges. Express appreciation and affection regularly to reinforce your bond and create positive energy.

- Understand that change is inevitable and embrace flexibility. Be willing to adapt to evolving circumstances and adjust expectations accordingly without negative emotions. Rigidity breeds resentment, while flexibility breeds harmony and cooperation.

- Prioritize self-care to maintain individual well-being and resilience. Nurture your physical, emotional, and spiritual health through practices such as exercise, meditation, hobbies, and time spent with loved ones. When you prioritize self-care, you bring your best self to the relationship. Fill your cup up so that you have plenty to share and spare.

- ❖ Conflict is not inherently detrimental; it's how you view it that matters. Approach disagreements with respect and a willingness to find common ground. Practice active listening, refrain from blame or defensiveness, and seek mutually beneficial solutions.

- ❖ Focus on appreciating the positive aspects of your relationship, even during challenging times. Cultivate gratitude for your partner's strengths, acts of kindness, and shared experiences. Gratitude supports love and understanding and deepens emotional connection.

- ❖ When needed, don't hesitate to seek support from trusted friends, family members, or relationship coaches. External perspective and guidance can offer invaluable insights and help you overcome and conquer complex issues more effectively.

- ❖ Establish healthy practices and routines that strengthen your connection and create shared meaning. Whether it's a weekly date night, morning rituals, or annual traditions, these practices provide stability and growth.

- ❖ View challenges as opportunities for growth and transformation. Instead of resisting difficulties, approach them as a mechanism for personal and relational evolution. Embrace the lessons they offer and emerge stronger together.

❖ Celebrate milestones and achievements, both big and small. Acknowledge progress, accomplishments, and moments of joy to reinforce positivity and reciprocate more.

Personal Insight: Establish silly and meaningful rituals, practices, or routines that honor your relationship's natural rhythms.

When you recognize, understand, and adapt to the natural rhythms of love inherent in this cosmic principle, you can forge a bond that is both timeless and eternal. You will discover the true essence of your partnership - a sacred union guided by the gentle rhythm of the heart. You can maintain stability and oneness by integrating these tools into your relationship.

∞∞∞

The Law of Rhythm also pertains to the ebb and flow of your life. Life's rhythm includes periods of rest and renewal, which encourages you to honor these essential phases. Being able to maintain equilibrium within yourself is crucial for being able to navigate it in your relationship. Consider the pause between musical notes, allowing for a full expression of the composition. Likewise, moments of rest allow you to replenish your energies, find balance, and restore well-being. The emotional well-being of you and your partner is equally important to the overall essence of your relationship. Recognizing the importance of rest and emotional balance within life's rhythm is a key aspect of conscious living. When you are hurting, you will unintentionally hurt those around you, usually the ones you love the most. This is why finding balance within yourself is crucial to the relationship. You can't give what you don't have.

Emotional balance is the basis of a healthy and thriving relationship. It encompasses practices and strategies that promote harmony and oneness. Emotional balance is essential for maintaining stability and grace.

- ❖ **Emotional Well-being** - Stability and grace contribute to the emotional well-being of you and your partner, establishing a sense of security, reassurance, and safety within your relationship. During challenging times, you may experience heightened levels of stress, anxiety, and uncertainty. Providing stability and grace creates a positive environment where emotions can be expressed and managed effectively, reducing the risk of emotional distress and instability. Practice mindful breathing, meditation, or any other exercise in this book that reduces stress and promotes emotional balance.

- ❖ **Emotional Resilience** - Stability and grace helps develop emotional resilience to withstand relationships' inevitable ups and downs. Develop practices such as meditation, self-reflection, and emotional regulation to work through challenging emotions. Emotional resilience empowers you and your partner to weather storms together.

- ❖ **Effective/Operational Communication** - Stability and grace facilitate effective/operational communication between you and your partner, enabling you to work through challenges and conflicts constructively. When you remain composed and considerate during difficult conversations and situations, you can express your thoughts, feelings, and concerns more clearly and empathetically.

- ❖ **Conflict Resolution** - Stability and grace are essential for successful conflict resolution. When you approach conflicts with patience, support, and honesty, you are better equipped to find mutually beneficial solutions and reach agreements that honor both partners' needs and preferences. Conversely, reactions fueled by anger, frustration, or defensiveness can escalate conflicts and undermine your efforts to resolve them.

- ❖ **Conflict Resolution Skills** - Stability and grace equip you with effective conflict resolution skills to address disagreements and misunderstandings constructively. Practice active listening, empathy, and cooperation to find mutually satisfactory solutions. Conflict resolution skills promote harmony and insight, mitigating the impact of conflicts on your relationship. These build understanding, validation, and togetherness, leading to resolutions that are mutually beneficial and sustainable.

- ❖ **Resilience and Adaptability** - Stability and grace contribute to your relationship's resilience and adaptability, enabling you to weather storms and emerge stronger from adversity. When you are faced with challenges and acquire strength, you demonstrate resilience by remaining steadfast in your commitment to your shared goals. This resilience enables you to adapt to changing circumstances, learn from setbacks, and grow individually and as a couple.

- ❖ **Modeling Healthy Behavior** - By embodying stability and grace during challenging times, you set a positive example for others to see and follow. Modeling healthy behavior demonstrates the importance of emotional intelligence, emotional regulation, and conflict resolution in maintaining a strong and durable relationship. This strengthens your bond and produces healthier relationship dynamics within your broader social circle.

- ❖ **Preservation of the Relationship** - Stability and grace serve as stabilizing forces during tumultuous periods, preventing conflicts from escalating and relationships from deteriorating. By maintaining a positive outlook and exhibiting compassion under pressure, you can preserve the integrity of your partnership and prevent irreparable damage.

- ❖ **Preservation of Intimacy and Connection** - Stability and grace are essential for preserving intimacy and connection. During challenging times, stress and conflict may cause increased emotional distance and disconnection. By maintaining stability and grace, you reestablish closeness, trust, and vulnerability, deepening your emotional ties and sustaining intimacy even in the face of adversity.

∞∞∞

The timeless secrets of maintaining stability and grace during challenging times are essential for preserving the integrity of your relationship. By promoting emotional well-being, facilitating effective communication and conflict resolution, building resilience and adaptability, modeling healthy behavior, and preserving intimacy and connection, you can create enduring love, which helps you move through challenging times with less strain and minimize extended periods of discord.

Relationship rhythm is characterized by constant change, and the Law of Rhythm encourages you to flow with these changes. Envision a river winding through diverse landscapes, adapting to the contours of its surroundings. This resembles your relationship's ebb and flow, which involves managing change with adaptability, patience, and flexibility. When you and your partner align yourselves with that rhythm of change, you can nurture positivity and remain open to the blessings that each phase brings. The Law of Rhythm facilitates this beauty of shared meaning and purpose within your relationship by encouraging you to evolve and grow together over time.

According to Rev. Shirley Lawson in *Golden Spiritual Nuggets*, "Dreams cannot become a reality if you remain asleep" (2009, p. 40).

Chapter Twelve
THE LAW OF GENDER
The Balance of Masculine and Feminine Energies in Relationships

In the final chapter of your exploration, you will focus on the wonderful Law of Gender. This law states that both masculine and feminine energies exist within all individuals, regardless of gender. These energies, often associated with traits stereotypically attributed to men and women, can play a significant role in shaping the dynamics of your relationship. Therefore, understanding and discovering the dynamics of these complementary energies within yourself and your partner is vital in pursuing a balanced and intimate relationship.

The Law of Gender is the last fundamental principle that we will cover overseeing your relationship. This law weighs the importance of identifying and allowing both your masculine and feminine energies into your experiences. The Law of Gender extends beyond your biological sex as it encompasses the balance of masculine and feminine energies within you. When you seek to understand and develop both your assertiveness/intellect (masculine) and nurturing/heart (feminine) qualities, you achieve a state of equilibrium and completeness.

THE LAW OF GENDER

Masculine energy, often associated with qualities such as strength, assertiveness, logic, and decisiveness, plays a pivotal role in your relationship. It's characterized by action-oriented behavior, goal-directedness, and problem-solving skills. In your relationship, masculine energy may manifest as providing protection, guidance, reasoning, and leadership, thereby promoting a sense of security and direction.

Feminine energy encompasses qualities such as empathy, intuition, nurturing, and receptivity. These are not just traits but powerful tools that can help you deeply understand and connect with your partner. Feminine energy is characterized by emotional intelligence, compassion, and the ability to connect deeply with others. In your relationship, feminine energy may manifest as nurturing care, emotional support, and intuitive understanding.

It's important to note that gender energies are not fixed or rigid; you possess varying degrees of both masculine and feminine qualities. These energies can ebb and flow depending on the context, circumstances, influences, and personal growth. Acknowledging the fluidity of gender energies empowers you to adapt and evolve together, embracing each other's changing needs and expressions.

∞∞∞

This law transcends physical attributes associated with gender, reaching into spiritual and energetic dimensions. Psychological studies on gender identity and the intersection of masculine and feminine qualities offer insights into the multifaceted nature of you. Research on the impact of gender stereotypes on relationship dynamics stresses the importance of transcending societal expectations and embracing the authentic expression of your masculine and feminine powers. Suppressing one and being overly skilled in the other creates a spiritual and physical imbalance. By examining the principles of gender, you begin to gain a deeper awareness of how your energies contribute to your holistic growth and relationship. Balanced relationships recognize and honor the qualities of both masculine and feminine energies in each partner to create equality and unity. By respecting the balance of your energies, you unlock your potential for creativity and transformation.

Gender is not merely a biological distinction; it encompasses a spectrum of traits, qualities, and energies. Masculine energy is often associated with assertiveness, logic, independence, and strength, while feminine energy is characterized by intuition, compassion, and nurturing. Both energies coexist and interact by influencing your communication, decision-making, and emotional expression in your relationship. Recognizing and appreciating these differences can further the understanding and cooperation between you and your partner. By acknowledging and using each partner's unique qualities, you can tap into the full spectrum of your human experiences, expanding your relationship with richness and completion.

Practical Insight: Explore and celebrate the unique strengths and qualities each partner brings to the relationship. Create an environment where each partner's masculine and feminine energies can coexist and complement each other in all areas of your relationship.

∞∞∞∞

You embody a unique combination of masculine and feminine energies, which influence the way you communicate, resolve conflict, and experience emotional intimacy. Let's explore how the balance of these energies impacts various aspects of your interactions.

Your masculine energy often drives direct, clear, and logical communication. It's focused on solving problems and getting to the point. On the other hand, your feminine energy brings empathy, intuition, and an understanding of unspoken emotions. When you balance these energies, your communication becomes both effective and compassionate. You can articulate your needs and thoughts clearly while also being sensitive to your partner's feelings, developing a more open and nurturing dialogue.

It's no secret that effective communication is essential for mutual understanding and resolving conflicts peacefully within your relationship. Your masculine energy may prioritize directness and problem-solving, while your feminine energy tends to emphasize empathy and emotional expression. By finding a balance between these energies - recognizing when and where you need to increase one and decrease the other - you uncover the secret to strengthening your ability to communicate effectively.

Practice active listening to engage your feminine energy and ensure you truly understand your partner's perspective. Simultaneously, use your masculine energy to express your thoughts and solutions confidently. This balance will enhance mutual understanding and reduce misunderstandings.

In conflict resolution, your masculine energy seeks to address the issue head-on, finding practical solutions quickly. Your feminine energy, however, encourages patience, understanding, and a deeper exploration of underlying issues. A balanced approach means you can address conflicts with both a problem-solving mindset and a compassionate heart, ensuring that both practical and emotional needs are met.

The correct combination of your masculine and feminine energies allows for a more collaborative approach when you contribute your strengths and perspectives to decision-making.

Your masculine energy excels in strategic planning and goal-setting, driving forward action and achieving tangible results. Meanwhile, your feminine energy adds depth through intuition, consideration of emotional implications, and a holistic view of situations.

Balancing these energies in decision-making ensures that your choices are not only logical and effective but also sensitive to your partner's feelings. Together, these energies facilitate informed decisions that align with your relationship's values and aspirations. Relying too heavily on one energy over the other creates an imbalance, taking you out of alignment and potentially producing negative effects.

When a conflict arises, take a moment to assess the situation. Use your masculine energy to identify the core issue and propose solutions, but also tap into your feminine energy to understand your partner's emotions and validate their feelings. This approach can prevent escalation and promote a more peaceful resolution.

In decision-making, engage both energies by setting clear goals and strategies (masculine) while also considering the emotional and relational impact of your decisions (feminine). This balanced approach will lead to more holistic and sustainable outcomes.

Masculine energy often expresses intimacy through actions and achievements, showing love through doing and providing. Feminine energy, conversely, expresses intimacy through emotional connection, nurturing, and shared feelings. Balancing these energies allows you to connect with your partner on both a physical and emotional level, deepening your bond and creating a more fulfilling relationship.

Emotional intimacy thrives when you feel loved, appreciated, and supported in your vulnerability. While your masculine energy may provide stability and protection, your feminine energy offers nurturing and empathy. By embracing and appreciating your unique vulnerabilities, you gain trust, enhance your emotional expression, and deepen your relationship.

Show your love through both actions and words. Plan meaningful activities together (masculine), take time to share your feelings, and listen to your partner's emotions (feminine). This dual approach will enhance your emotional intimacy and strengthen your relationship as your partner begins to see you as a balanced and fully-rounded individual.

Operating predominantly from one energy over the other creates an imbalance, which can manifest as miscommunication, unresolved conflicts, and emotional disconnect. By cultivating both your masculine and feminine energies, you align with the natural dualities within yourself and your relationship, promoting harmony and growth.

Practical Insight: Embrace and strive to develop both energies within you. Acknowledge that strength lies in the ability to be both assertive and compassionate, logical and intuitive. By honoring and integrating these energies, you create a dynamic, resilient relationship capable of weathering challenges and thriving in love.

Practical Steps

- ❖ Reflect on which energy you predominantly use and in which situations. Aim to recognize and honor the presence of both energies within you.

- ❖ Engage in activities that nurture both energies, such as meditation (feminine) and goal-setting exercises (masculine).

- ❖ Encourage your partner to explore and balance their energies as well. Support each other in this journey of self-discovery and relational growth.

- ❖ Regularly discuss with your partner how you both can better balance these energies in your relationship.

By understanding and balancing your masculine and feminine energies, you achieve internal balance, creating a relationship that is not only harmonious but also rich in depth and mutual respect.

THE LAW OF GENDER

Hermeticism, a philosophical system dating back to ancient Egypt and Greece, outlines several universal laws governing existence. One of these principles is the Law of Gender, which teaches that everything contains both masculine and feminine elements. These energies are not confined to physical gender but represent different qualities and forces.

According to Hermetic philosophy, the interplay between these energies is essential for creation and balance. Both are necessary, and neither is superior to the other. They complement each other, creating a dynamic balance within you that supports growth and harmony.

Masculine energy is often associated with leadership, action-oriented, and decisiveness. It embodies traits such as independence, rationality, and competitiveness. Whereas feminine energy encompasses patience, emotional expression, and receptivity. It includes qualities like patience, creativity, and softness.

Gender dynamics shape the dynamics of your relationship in profound ways. Societal norms, cultural expectations, and personal experiences shape how you express your masculine and feminine energies. These energies are not opposing forces but complementary aspects that, when balanced, create unity. Misalignment or imbalance in your dynamics can lead to misunderstandings, conflicts, and emotional disconnection. By recognizing the impact of your gender dynamics, you can tap into the power of your combined energies for the overall betterment of your relationship. This allows you to express and appreciate qualities traditionally associated with both your masculine and feminine energies.

In your daily life and relationship, understanding and balancing these energies can lead to more satisfying interactions and higher levels of self-esteem and adaptability. When you achieve a balance between these energies, you create a more integrated and harmonious sense of self, which contributes to healthier self-esteem. Here are some ways you can recognize and balance your masculine and feminine energies and boost your self-esteem.

- ❖ Embracing Your Full Self
    - ➢ By acknowledging and integrating both masculine and feminine traits, you accept all aspects of your personality. This acceptance establishes a sense of wholeness and self-acceptance, which is crucial for high self-esteem.

- ❖ Enhanced Self-Awareness
    - ➢ Balancing these energies increases self-awareness, helping you better understand your strengths and weaknesses. This self-awareness allows you to make more informed decisions and act in ways that align with your true self, boosting your confidence.

- ❖ Improved Relationships
    - ➢ Balanced energies lead to healthier relationships because you can empathize, communicate effectively, and assert your needs without dominating others. Positive relationships reinforce your sense of worth and value, enhancing your self-esteem.

- ❖ Emotional Stability
  - ➤ Balancing masculine and feminine energies helps you manage your emotions better. You can express your feelings (feminine) and take constructive action (masculine) without being overwhelmed by either. This emotional stability builds resilience and self-confidence.

- ❖ Increased Resilience
  - ➤ When you balance assertiveness with empathy, you become more resilient in the face of challenges. You can face difficulties head-on (masculine) while also nurturing yourself and seeking support when needed (feminine). This resilience reinforces your belief in your ability to overcome obstacles, boosting your self-esteem.

- ❖ Empowered Decision-Making
  - ➤ Balancing analytical thinking with intuition enables you to make well-rounded decisions. You trust your judgment and instincts, leading to more successful outcomes and a stronger sense of self-assurance.

- ❖ Authentic Expression
  - ➤ Balancing energies allows you to express yourself authentically. You are neither suppressing your emotional side nor neglecting your logical side. This authenticity fosters self-respect and esteem as you live true to who you are.

- ❖ Fulfillment and Purpose
  - ➢ When your actions (masculine) are aligned with your values and emotions (feminine), you feel a greater sense of purpose and fulfillment. This alignment enhances your overall satisfaction with life, contributing to higher self-esteem.

Practical Steps

- ❖ Begin by identifying the predominant energy within yourself. Are you more inclined towards assertiveness and action, or do you lean towards empathy and intuition? Understanding your natural tendencies is the first step in achieving balance.

- ❖ Regularly assess your actions and feelings to understand which energy is dominating and why.

- ❖ Effective communication requires a blend of both energies. Your masculine energy can help you express your needs clearly and assertively, while your feminine energy allows you to listen empathetically and respond with compassion.

- ❖ During conflicts, balancing these energies can lead to peaceful resolutions. The masculine approach focuses on solving the problem directly, while the feminine approach emphasizes understanding and emotional connection. Combining both can help you address the issue while maintaining emotional intimacy.

- ❖ Engage in mindfulness or meditation to cultivate a balance between your analytical and intuitive sides.

- ❖ Work on developing emotional intelligence by recognizing and managing your emotions effectively. Balance your actions and emotions, ensuring you are not overly harsh or too emotional to see the entire picture.

- ❖ Develop emotional intimacy by embracing your feminine energy to nurture and connect with your partner on a deeper level. Simultaneously, use your masculine energy to create a safe and secure environment for open expression.

- ❖ Set and respect personal boundaries to protect your emotional well-being.

- ❖ Engage in activities that nurture both energies, like creative pursuits (feminine) and strategic planning (masculine).

∞∞∞

Research in psychology and gender studies provides valuable information on how balancing masculine and feminine energies can impact relationships and individual well-being. For instance, studies have found that individuals who exhibit a balance of traditionally masculine and feminine traits tend to have higher levels of self-esteem and adaptability. Whereas couples who practice balancing these energies report higher relationship satisfaction. And in the workplace, embracing both energies can lead to better leadership and teamwork.

Where are you on the spectrum?

Practical Applications

Balancing masculine and feminine energies is a practical approach to improving your life and relationships. Here are some strategies to apply this principle.

Practice mindfulness to become more aware of your internal energies. Meditation can help you connect with both your masculine and feminine sides, supporting inner balance.

Reflect on your experiences and behaviors through journaling. Identify situations where you exhibited more masculine or feminine energy and consider how you could balance them better.

Seeking guidance from a therapist or coach can help you explore and balance these energies. Professionals can provide tools and techniques to integrate both energies effectively. Go to www.legendaryrelationship.com to review our coaching opportunities and therapy referrals.

Continuously educate yourself about gender dynamics and personal development. Books, workshops, and courses on gender balance and relationship skills can provide valuable insights and practices. Go to www.legendaryrelationship.com to review other books, coaching, courses, workshops, and more.

The Law of Gender teaches that balance between masculine and feminine energies is crucial for serenity, unity, and happiness in your life and relationship. By understanding and integrating these energies, you can enhance your communication, conflict resolution, and emotional intimacy, to assist you

THE LAW OF GENDER

in manifesting your desired relationship. Adopt this ancient wisdom to create a balanced and harmonious life, where both your masculine and feminine sides are valued and nurtured.

∞∞∞

The Law of Gender prompts an understanding of the archetypal qualities associated with your masculine and feminine energies. Consider the sun and the moon as archetypal symbols - the sun represents active, assertive, and outward-focused masculine energy, while the moon embodies receptive, nurturing, and inwardly reflective feminine energy. Both these energies are essential for the vitality and balance of creation.

To harmonize your masculine and feminine energies within your relationship, acknowledge and balance the inner integration of both aspects of your nature. Establishing cooperative approaches between you and your partner, coupled with an appreciation for each other's unique qualities, can serve to be a vital tool for nurturing equilibrium and synergy within your partnership.

Embracing diversity in gender expression requires a willingness to challenge traditional stereotypes and roles. By consciously incorporating both masculine and feminine qualities into your interactions, you can create a balanced partnership. Depending on the context, this may involve practicing empathy, vulnerability, and assertiveness interchangeably. By embracing flexibility and adaptability, you can support mutual empowerment.

∞∞∞

Love is the binding essence between you and your partner. It thrives when you harmoniously integrate the energies of the Law of Gender. Each partner brings a distinct blend of masculine and feminine qualities to the relationship, creating a synergistic environment where love can flourish. By recognizing and appreciating these qualities in each other, you deepen your emotional ties, introducing ever-evolving love into your bond.

Practical Insight: Engaging in activities that allow each partner to express their masculine and feminine energies can enrich the relationship. For example, partners may take turns planning dates (representing masculine energy) and creating moments of emotional intimacy (reflecting feminine energy), thereby nurturing a rich and fulfilling connection that embraces both aspects of the self.

Jason's Account:

I remember a time when our beloved Uncle Nelson came to visit. The yard looked perfect, with flowers in full bloom around all of our ten trees, and along the perimeter of the house and pond, the fence, and on both sides of our shed. Our wood floors were shining like new money, reflecting the beautiful sunlight streaming through the window. After finishing his breakfast, Uncle Nelson took a stroll outside to admire the flowers. A few minutes later, he returned and complimented me on what a great job I had done on the floors and how beautiful Tina's flowers were. Tina and I ecstatically laughed as I told him that Tina had done the floors and I had taken care of the flowers.

Typical stereotypical roles have never been our thing. Throughout our relationship, those who are not open and balanced in their own masculine and feminine energies have tried to tell us how we should be in our relationship - how Tina should be doing a, b, and c while I should be doing x, y, and z. However, we have never had a problem being secure in our own masculine and feminine energies, which adds to the uniqueness and richness of our relationship. But we did have to learn how to balance our personal and relationship energies. By nurturing and balancing our energies through the practices in this book, we have found that this contributes to creating balance in our relationship - I'm her yin, and she's, my yang.

By implementing these practical strategies and embracing the principles of the Law of Gender, you will improve the balance of masculine and feminine energies in your relationship. This holistic approach promotes understanding, appreciation, and synergy for longevity and enduring connection grounded in authenticity and mutual growth.

The Law of Gender underscores the significance of both masculine and feminine energies in the creative process. Just as a seed planted in fertile soil symbolizes the union of masculine and feminine elements initiating life's germination, creation in various realms - be it physical, emotional, or spiritual - requires the harmonious collaboration of these energies. This creative union is evident in the birth of ideas, relationships, and transformative experiences, highlighting the profound impact of embracing diverse energies within partnerships.

In relationships, you may find that one person acknowledges they are not creative or have other perceived shortcomings. This presents a significant opportunity for you to build relational value by developing a balance of your masculine and feminine energies. If your partner has strengths in areas where you feel less confident, view this as a chance to work together and help each other nurture those particular areas. Instead of seeing each other's strengths and weaknesses as positive or negative, embrace them as opportunities for improving support by building and strengthening your connection.

∞∞∞

Realize that gender-related challenges may manifest in various forms, such as communication barriers, power struggles, or rigid gender roles. These challenges can undermine trust, intimacy, and overall relationship satisfaction. It's essential for you and your partner to identify and address these issues proactively rather than allowing them to fester and escalate. Open and honest communication, linked with cooperation and clear expectations, can help you overcome these obstacles together. The goal is to use these laws and tools to bridge your separateness.

Differences in your communication styles between masculine and feminine energies can lead to disagreements and disputes. These contrasting styles can result in communication breakdowns if not effectively addressed. You may encounter struggles if you and your partner share the same communication style. Understand your style and how to balance it for improving your communication.

Gender dynamics often influence power dynamics within relationships, with traditional norms positioning men as dominant and women as passive. These power imbalances can manifest in controlling behaviors, decision-making disparities, and emotional manipulation. Overcoming this challenge requires a shift towards egalitarianism, where both partners share power and decision-making responsibilities. Building mutual respect, trust, and cooperation is essential in rebalancing power dynamics within your relationship. Remember the importance of both you and your partner being allowed to express your own uniqueness and find a balance in your energies that works for your relationship. Over-dominating or controlling behavior is a clear indication of energy imbalance.

Societal norms often discourage men from expressing vulnerability and emotions, equating them with weakness. This reluctance to be vulnerable can hinder emotional intimacy and connection within your relationship. Conversely, women may feel pressure to prioritize emotional caretaking over their own needs. Overcoming these challenges involves creating a safe space for emotional expression and vulnerability, where you and your partner feel seen, heard, and accepted without judgment or stigma.

Gender norms may dictate how you express and perceive your emotions, with masculine energy often associated with stoicism and emotional restraint, while feminine energy is associated with vulnerability and emotional openness. Overcoming these stereotypes allows you to cultivate emotional intimacy, trust, and authenticity.

Masculine and feminine energies may influence how you approach conflict resolution. Masculine energy may gravitate towards direct confrontation and problem-solving, while feminine energy may prefer indirect communication and empathy. Understanding and respecting each other's conflict styles can prevent escalation and promote resolution.

Gender dynamics can shape communication patterns within your relationship, influencing aspects such as tone, body language, and verbal cues. Effective communication requires active listening, empathy, and mutual respect, transcending gender stereotypes for genuine understanding and connection.

Cultural and familial influences can shape your perceptions and expectations regarding gender roles and dynamics within your relationship. Cultural norms may vary widely, impacting communication styles, decision-making processes, and relationship expectations. Familial upbringing also plays a significant role, as you may unconsciously replicate patterns observed in your parents' relationship. Overcoming this challenge requires awareness and critical reflection on cultural and familial influences, allowing you to consciously choose values and dynamics that align with your relationship goals.

Recognizing the multifaceted nature of masculine and feminine energies and exploring their impact on your relationship dynamics can bring greater awareness, kindness, and patience to your intimate union. Recognizing communication styles, gender dynamics, challenging societal norms, gender norms, approach to conflict resolution, communication patterns, cultural and familial influences, and embracing diversity allows you and your partner to manifest a partnership characterized by your shared vision and love.

∞∞∞

Gender-related conflicts are common in relationships. To navigate these conflicts, establish clear roles and responsibilities for each partner, and don't assume your partner knows what you think and expect, even if it seems evident to you.

THE LAW OF GENDER

Understanding the influence of gender dynamics on your self-perception and interaction with your partner is crucial. The Law of Gender describes your masculine and feminine energies as a spectrum of qualities and traits you inherit, regardless of your biological sex. Embracing these energies can help you navigate and overcome gender-related conflicts in your relationship.

When actively listening to your partner, it's essential to pay attention to both verbal and nonverbal cues. But more than that, strive to empathize with their perspectives.

Expressing your needs, boundaries, and concerns in a clear and respectful manner is key. Assertiveness fosters transparency and mutual understanding, which in turn reduces misunderstandings and resentment. Providing constructive feedback to address issues and improve communication, while focusing on specific behaviors or actions rather than personal attacks, is also important.

Utilize conflict resolution strategies to navigate disagreements and reach mutually satisfactory outcomes. But remember, these strategies should always be underpinned by mutual respect. By focusing on shared goals and values, you can promote effective conflict resolution and ensure that both you and your partner feel valued and appreciated. This, in turn, can help reduce future conflicts.

∞∞∞∞

Metaphysics examines the fundamental nature of reality, encompassing the relationship between mind and matter, substance and attribute, and potentiality and actuality. The American philosopher and psychologist William James defined metaphysics as "Nothing but an unusually obstinate effort to think clearly."

In metaphysical philosophy, the interplay between masculine and feminine energies is front and center in your relationship, determining the perceived aspects between you and your partner. Within this philosophical framework, the concepts of masculine and feminine energies extend beyond physical characteristics, symbolizing essential aspects of your human conscious and subconscious mind, influencing how you connect and grow together. Understanding and balancing these energies can lead to profound personal and relational growth on spiritual, mental, and universal levels.

Masculine energy is traditionally associated with your conscious mind and thinking nature. It embodies qualities such as reason, choose, examine, judge, analyze, will, select, decide, evaluate, deduct, form, reject, accept, and conclude (UFBL/JCTS Illustration, n.d.). This energy drives your desire to explore, conquer, and create order in your relationship. It is forward-moving, characterized by clarity, direction, and the pursuit of goals. Your conscious mind, governed by masculine energy, becomes the seat of rational thought, decision-making, and conscious awareness.

Conversely, feminine energy is linked to your subconscious mind and feeling nature. It represents memory, experience, observations, emotions, mood, temperament, attitude of mind, and accumulated knowledge (UFBL/JCTS Illustration, n.d.). Feminine energy is fluid, adaptive, and introspective, guiding you through the inner world of emotions and subconscious processes. It is the source of your creativity, empathy, and the ability to connect deeply with your partner. Infused with feminine energy, your subconscious mind holds the reservoir of memories, dreams, and intrinsic motivations.

The distinction between masculine and feminine energies in metaphysical philosophy goes beyond physical gender and touches on the intrinsic qualities and states of being that you possess. Regardless of your gender, you embody both masculine and feminine energies. The balance of these energies is essential for holistic well-being and growth in your relationship. When these energies harmonize, you experience equilibrium that enhances your ability to navigate relationship challenges with greater wisdom and compassion.

Balancing masculine and feminine energies involves integrating the conscious and subconscious aspects of your mind. This integration leads to a more profound understanding of yourself and your partner. This balance allows you to make more effective decisions, build emotional resilience, and create meaningful connections with your partner.

Balancing this energy is essential for achieving peace and harmony in your relationship. Finding balance within yourself transforms the circumstances and events in your life, directly impacting how you interact with your partner. Relying excessively on either emotion (feminine) or intellect (masculine) can hinder your growth and weaken your relationship.

The only place you can truly find this balance is within your consciousness. When you stress your intellect or emotions too much, it becomes easy to lose balance. When not in harmony, intellect and emotions pull you off-center, disrupting your inner equilibrium. Functioning with rational awareness and emotional stability keeps you centered and balanced, which is crucial for maintaining a healthy and harmonious relationship.

When you let your emotions completely manipulate you, your judgment becomes clouded, leading to disharmony in your relationship. You might react impulsively, misinterpret your partner's actions, or struggle to communicate effectively. Similarly, if you are prone to overanalyze things, you can become stuck in a cycle of excessive rationality, preventing you from connecting emotionally with your partner. Overanalyzing can lead to indecisiveness, mistrust, and an inability to enjoy the present moment.

Your subconscious mind plays a vital role in maintaining balance. Whatever you hold in your subconscious influences your body and your actions. Thoughts are the mental activities that build consciousness, forming the basis of your conscious mind. You are completely responsible for the thoughts you hold and how you use them. Positive, balanced thoughts contribute to a healthy, balanced state of consciousness, while negative or imbalanced thoughts can lead to disharmony.

Inner balance is a prerequisite for peace and harmony in your relationship (Warch, 1977/2016). To achieve this balance, you should start by cultivating awareness of both your masculine and feminine energies. Recognize when you are overly reliant on your intellect or emotions and make a conscious effort to bring them into balance. Practice mindfulness and self-reflection to understand your thought patterns and emotional responses. By doing so, you can create a stable foundation within yourself that supports a harmonious relationship with your partner.

Spiritually, the balance of masculine and feminine energies aligns with the concept of unity and oneness in your relationship. Many spiritual traditions emphasize the importance of transcending dualities to achieve enlightenment or self-realization. By embracing both energies, you and your partner move beyond the limitations of rigid gender roles and societal expectations, creating a more inclusive and expansive spiritual perspective within your relationship.

Mentally, this balance enhances your cognitive and emotional functioning. The analytical competence of masculine energy, combined with the creative and intuitive strengths of feminine energy, results in a more holistic approach to problem-solving and innovation in your relationship. Emotional intelligence, a key component of mental health, is significantly enhanced when you are attuned to both your rational and emotional selves.

Universally, balancing masculine and feminine energies contributes to a more harmonious and interconnected relationship. As you improve this balance within yourself, you become better equipped to contribute positively to your relationship and the broader human collective. This harmony adds greater empathy, cooperation, and understanding, which are essential for addressing challenges and creating a more equitable and compassionate world together.

When you balance your masculine and feminine energies, you can approach your relationship with both rational awareness and emotional stability. You will be able to communicate effectively, make thoughtful decisions, and respond to your partner's needs with empathy and understanding. This balance allows you to work through the complexities of your relationship with greater ease and grace. When you are centered and balanced, you are better equipped to handle challenges, support your partner, and build a strong, resilient relationship.

The metaphysical concept of masculine and feminine energies offers an understanding of the dynamics of your conscious and subconscious mind in your intimate relationship. Balancing masculine and feminine energies within yourself is crucial for achieving peace and love in your relationship. Maintaining rational awareness and emotional stability creates a balanced state of consciousness that promotes personal and relational growth. Remember, the journey to balance begins within your own consciousness, and you have the power to create a loving relationship by developing this inner equilibrium. The balance of masculine and feminine energies is not only a pathway to individual well-being but also a catalyst for spiritual, mental, and universal accord in your intimate relationships.

"Until you make the unconscious conscious, it will direct your life and you will call it fate." — Carl Jung

Carl Jung's quote captures the need for self-awareness and the integration of unconscious elements into conscious understanding. This aligns perfectly with the metaphysical philosophy of balancing masculine and feminine energies within yourself to achieve inner peace and relational harmony. By making the unconscious conscious, you can prevent it from inadvertently steering your life, thus taking active control of your personal and relational growth.

∞∞∞∞∞

To manifest a joy-filled relationship, you must recognize a force larger than yourself at play in the universe. This book has guided you to understand that the universe operates in the background, influencing your relationship and personal journey. Realize that change starts with you; to alter your external circumstances, you must first evolve internally. Your self-improvement directly impacts the quality of your relationships and overall life.

The essence of this journey is self-evolution. As you become a better individual, every aspect of your life, including your relationships, will improve. This book emphasizes that you have the power to align yourself with the universal laws, enabling you to manifest your desires through your thoughts. Thoughts held in mind produce after their kind, and you have the choice to cultivate positive, constructive thoughts.

You are part of a universal oneness, connected through the energy that composes the universe. This energy is malleable, and you have the power to shape it according to your desires. The true power lies within you, not outside. It is your internal state, your thoughts, and your feelings that determine your reality.

From the foundational Law of Divine Oneness to the subtle dance of masculine and feminine energies in the Law of Gender, each law contributes to an awareness that helps guide you toward a happy and truly fulfilling connection. It is crucial to be aware of your alignment with your desires. Understand where you might be out of sync and what steps are needed to realign. Your thinking and feeling must be in harmony to create the changes you wish to see. Correct thinking from the head, combined with the right feelings from the heart, leads to perfect alignment, enabling you to manifest your desires. Don't just be a mere spectator; be an active participant in learning, using, and applying this knowledge to manifest your desired relationship.

As the Rev. Dr. Johnnie Colemon would always remind us, it works if you work it! But the real truth lies in the working part. Nothing happens by chance; it happens by choice. You have the choice to intentionally co-create your relationship or let other factors or situations in the universe decide for you.

Choose to make the right decisions by aligning your thoughts and feelings with universal laws, becoming the architect of a joyous relationship. There is no such thing as luck; co-create with full awareness of the power you possess!

From *What We Believe* by Don Nedd, commentary by Helen W. Carry, "We believe that a mighty new wind is blowing. Men everywhere are hungry for practical techniques that will show them how to fulfill the good desires of their hearts. We in the U.F.B.L. believe that we have these techniques and we offer them to everyone without distinction, confident that with the help of the Holy Spirit, we can teach all who are willing to learn how to overcome whatever would keep them from their highest good." (Nedd, 1990, p. 11).

ABOUT THE AUTHORS

Certified Life and Relationship Coaches Jason and Tina Marie Scott have been married for thirty-three years and are proud parents of three amazing young adults. They are the founders of Legendary Relationship and hosts of the global weekly podcast Loving Beyond The I Do.

They are on a mission to transform lives by teaching people how to create joyous relationships through right thinking, words, feelings, actions, and reactions that reflect unconditional love and dedication. Known as the "Dynamic Duo in Marriage" they are, undoubtedly, "In It to Win It!"

Works Cited

Angelou, Maya. *Wouldn't Take Nothing for My Journey Now*. Random House, 1993.

Burton, Neel. "My Top-12 Jung Quotations." *Psychology Today*, Sussex Publishers, 14 July 2019, www.psychologytoday.com/us/blog/hide-and-seek/201204/jung-the-man-and-his-symbols. Updated June 2024. Accessed June 2024.

Chapman, Gary. *The Five Love Languages: How to Express Heartfelt Commitment to Your Mate*. Northfield Publishing, 2015.

Drucker, Peter F. *The Effective Executive: The Definitive Guide to Getting the Right Things Done*. Harper & Row, 1966.

Einstein, Albert. "In the middle of difficulty lies opportunity." *The Ultimate Quotable Einstein*, edited by Alice Calaprice, Princeton University Press, 2011, p. 480.

Fillmore, Charles. *The Revealing Word: A Dictionary of Metaphysical Terms*. Unity School of Christianity, 1959. Reprint, Martino Publishing, 2014.

Glasow, Arnold H. *The Glassow's Business Book*. Morrow, 1985.

Jerry Maguire. Directed by Cameron Crowe, performances by Tom Cruise, Renée Zellweger, and Cuba Gooding Jr., TriStar Pictures, 1996.

Johnnie Colemon Institute. *Basic Principles Worksheet*. Johnnie Colemon Institute, n.d.

Lao Tzu. *Tao Te Ching*. Translated by Stephen Mitchell, Harper Perennial, 1988.

Lawson, Rev. Shirley. *Golden Spiritual Nuggets*. Self-Published, 2009.

Nedd, Don, and Helen W. Carry. *What We Believe*. Universal Foundation for Better Living, Inc., 1990.

Nietzsche, Friedrich. *Human, All Too Human.* Translated by Helen Zimmern, Macmillan, 1909.

St. Francis Prayer, The." Make Me an Instrument of Your Peace. Amazon, www.amazon.com/Prayer-St-Francis-Assisi-MAGNET/dp/B08231PGQW. Accessed 6 Dec. 2023.

Teresa, Mother. *A Gift for God: Prayers and Meditations.* Harper & Row, 1975.

Tolle, Eckhart. *The Power of Now: A Guide to Spiritual Enlightenment.* New World Library, 1999.

Warch, William. *New Thought Christian: An Introduction to the Life-Changing Concepts of New Thought.* 1977. Reprint, DeVorss & Company, 2016.

LET'S START MANIFESTING NOW

For discounted bulk purchases of this book for your company, association, or conference, please email us at

team@legendaryrelationship.com

To book Jason and Tina Marie for interviews or speaking visit legendaryrelationship.com or contact

team@legendaryrelationship.com

For more books, resources, and support visit

www.legendaryrelationship.com

Connect with us

Website: legendaryrelationship.com

Email: team@legendaryrelationship.com

YouTube: youtube.com/@legendaryrelationship

Instagram: instagram.com/legendaryrelationship

TikTok: tiktok.com/@legendaryrelationship

Facebook: facebook.com/legendaryrelationship

Podcast: Loving Beyond The I Do

To support book donations to churches, libraries, and non-profit organizations visit:
www.manifestajoyfilledrelationship.com

PLEASE LEAVE A REVIEW

www.legendaryrelationship.com/manifestreview

www.ingramcontent.com/pod-product-compliance
Lightning Source LLC
Chambersburg PA
CBHW020655060526
44119CB00068B/7